SILK
PAINTING

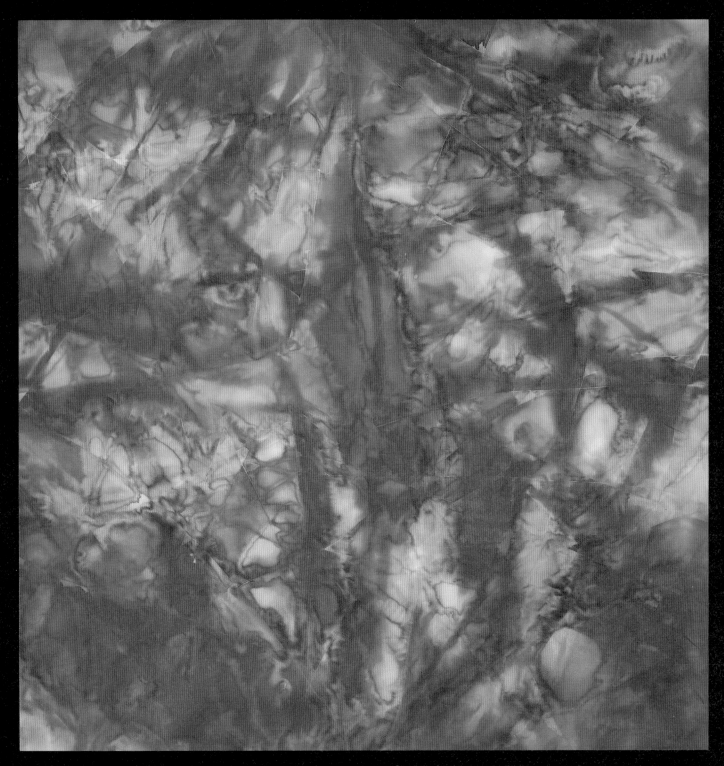

Opal fire depicted on translucent silk

SILK
PAINTING

Techniques
and projects

Compiled by Di Teasdale

ROBERT HALE • LONDON

Designed by Barbara Beckett Publishing

© *Di Teasdale 1991*
First published in Great Britain 1992

ISBN-0-7090-4874-2

Robert Hale Limited
Clerkenwell House
Clerkenwell Green
London EC1R OHT

Printed in Hong Kong by Colorcraft Ltd

Contents

Left: Dawn,
beginning of time *by*
Louise Feneley

Right: Callistemon –
Australian bottlebrush

*Special thanks to my husband Ray
and daughter-in-law Helen, for their
help and encouragement during the
preparation for this book.*

Foreword

DI TEASDALE is one of those enviable people who have a natural talent, that in-built sense of line and colour and the ability to reproduce her creative thoughts in the medium of her choice. That is not to say that it all comes easily to this versatile artist. Not by any means! She actually works at it. Many hours of planning and preparation go into her artistic endeavours and the resultant pieces are evidence of this.

I have known Di as an exciting and meticulous porcelain artist, a very dear friend and more recently as an enthusiastic and dynamic painter with silk as her latest medium. This difficult and often treacherous 'canvas' has provided her with a challenging vehicle which is stimulating and adventurous. Her explorations into the diverse pleasures of colour and natural fibre, mastering their unruly union, governing the direction of design and controlling the passage of the dye, have produced exciting compositions with impressive intensity of colour. Her wonderful naturalistic representations of wildlife, so realistically portrayed on porcelain, are now featured in this delightful medium along with contemporary designs and modern linear construction.

Always generous with her knowledge, Di once again has shared with us the results of her labours. In the following pages she has detailed for us the materials she finds most useful, the various techniques of application and many new methods of presentation. Her instructions are clear and concise, easily understood by the novice, readily adapted by the practising artist and provide all who read them with a wealth of ideas and enthusiasm.

This is a refreshing book of instruction which will provide readers with many hours of enjoyment and pleasure as they put into practice the delightful art of painting on silk.

Tricia Bradford

Introduction

Silk painting began for me as an adjunct to something else I was doing. Like most people who become hooked on a particular art, craft or hobby I felt the limitless dimensions and extreme subtleties of my particular love were only really understood by the already initiated.

At the time I was involved in a three-woman show in which we were to exhibit in several mediums, proving that while we could be 'real artists' in a more acceptable medium, we chose to express ourselves on porcelain.

Life is strange; one goes off on a tangent for whatever reasons only to discover a path which, in hindsight, was probably inevitable. A sort of natural evolvement. This particular change of direction I trusted because it felt right.

Silk felt right. The colour, translucence, the unpredictable qualities of this fantastic canvas had me spellbound.

That was four years ago. The medium is not so wildly unpredictable because my technique has improved, but the enthusiasm is the same. These days some of what is in my head actually goes down onto the silk. However, usually the best bits are where the silk, rejecting my limitations, has taken its own line. Small wonder silk painting is addictive.

I was soon to discover my addiction was not unique and that many methods exist for converting a shimmering white mass of silk to vivid colour. For each silk method there are people committed to practising that particular art form.

I have been fortunate to be able to draw together the experiences of some of these talented artists to illustrate a variety of silk painting techniques, which are practised in Australia today. My apologies to the exponents of other techniques not featured in this book. For the technically minded there are chapters dealing with dyestuff, silk the fibre, silk the cloth and its history. This research has been provided by a respected authority on the subject who is unfortunate enough to be a friend. 'Wearable art' features strongly throughout this book so that chapters by a creative quilter seemed appropriate. Great ideas and helpful hints have been wrought from hard experience.

My thanks to these talented individuals who have given generously of their time and energy to write and illustrate chapters for this book, outlining their particular techniques, sharing their thoughts and giving insight into their own silk experience.

Di Teasdale

Left: Kaleidoscopic panorama

Right: One dream has to lead to another.

1

The love of colour

Louise Feneley

*B*ORN *in 1949, Louise graduated from the South Australian School of Art in 1970. At this time she was awarded the Ailsa Osborne Art Gallery Prize for composition.*

From then until 1986 she worked with oils, pastel and water colour having many group and solo exhibitions in South Australia and Western Australia. She also taught painting and drawing to adults and children.

In 1986 she moved into working on silk which enabled her to build on her established skills of colour and design with a new medium, and renewed inspiration.

I HAVE always loved the hills and forests, the sea, sand, rocks, clouds, trees, streams, flowers, shells, feathers—all those delightful things of nature, large and small, that as an artist I treasure. So naturally, these have been the source of my inspiration. The beauty of nature is never failing, is always there like a trusted friend that one can turn to when one's creative energy seems low.

Thankfully I am the type of person who can stand (or sit) and look, observe and look some more at a leaf, sunset, clouds or a misty morning, taking it all in, remembering the colours or just meditating on its beauty. I think the quality of being acutely aware of one's surroundings, the colours, atmosphere, shapes, patterns and textures, is essential, for it sharpens the imagination and gives plenty of inner pictures to draw from later when inspiration is needed.

I remember as a child running my eyes around the edges of things in my room like the lamp, chair, desk, shoes, anything and everything. This was perhaps an early lesson in drawing because I was learning something about the forms of those subjects.

Drawing, the ability to observe and record form, light and shade, is as necessary to the art of painting on silk as to any other art form. It takes practice to bring out the essence of a subject and at times it takes patience and persistence to reach a successful conclusion.

My greatest delight in painting on silk has been to have a ball with colour. Using the clear bright colours of the spectrum is healing for the soul and in fact I have noticed I often subconsciously choose to use the colours my being is most in need of at the time.

The muted, more subtle colours I find relaxing and they bring me closer to the element of earth, whereas the pale tones of the spectrum seem to relate to the element of air, lightness and ethereal subjects.

Any mood one wishes to create can be brought about by one's choice of colour and tone. Softness, lightness, sweetness, femininity seem to call for peachy pinks and apricot tones, pale blues and mauves or very light yellows. A jazzy flavour can be expressed by the juxtaposition of many different bright complementaries; a mysterious quality can be brought out by the use of violet blues darkening almost to black, purples with perhaps an accent of scarlet.

Colour alone can work miracles!

The designing of fabric calls for an eye for pattern. Everywhere one looks interesting patterns present themselves—tyre marks in the sand, the shadows of long grass, the repeat pattern of a fence or the windowed wall of a high rise building, patterns in a receding tide, feathers, shells, trees in a forest, balloons in a park, umbrellas on a beach.

Looking at familiar objects or sights through new or different eyes, one can find unexpected and interesting shapes, patterns and textures. Looking at something upside down or reflected in a mirror can reveal new aspects.

Painting on silk is a 'direct' method as it is not easy to remove dye or gutta once it's on. I basically decide what I'm going to do and how I'm going to do it before I put any gutta or colour onto the silk. In this way I can work confidently and purposefully to complete my task before the dye dries.

At times inspiration can be an elusive experience. Someone asked me, 'How do I get inspired?' 'How do I find out what I want to paint?'

Inspiration is a state of mind, a state of being, like meditation or falling in love. It's a state that needs cultivation, which means putting aside daily troubles, the small things that don't really matter in relation to eternity, and musing on, feeling into those things that mean most, that one feels passionate about or loves. The work arising from this will not be simply an exercise but an experience.

To me art is a reverberation of the inner beauty of an object, person or situation. Rembrandt said that a painting will exhale joy, if he, as the artist 'laughs in his soul while painting'.

Wayside brambles

Left: Winter rockwater

Right: Flinders Ranges memory

2
Pictures in silk

Beverley Ambridge

Born in Adelaide and a graduate of Adelaide Teachers College, Beverley taught art in secondary schools for some time before travelling to London.

Here she worked as an artist/designer to a badge-maker until she returned to Australia to become artist/researcher to the House of Heraldry.

Beverley is best known, however, as a fine artist and teacher of porcelain art specialising in the field of innovative overglaze technique.

AS WITH MOST art experiences in my life, silk painting was yet another that I became involved in almost by chance.

For many years my favourite medium was china painting or on-glaze decoration. One afternoon I sat between two friends who were talking excitedly about a proposed silk workshop. I became caught up in the conversation and decided that I was missing out on this new art form. I too bought an apron and joined in.

I must now pay tribute to the author and compiler of this book. If ever a group had a more generous, zany, inventive and talented teacher I've yet to meet him or her. The bulk of my group were china decorators—a very controlled medium—and here we were suddenly swept into the vagaries of silk whose charm lies in its inability to be controlled. Within hours I had recoloured my new apron, stained my arms to the elbows and poured an entire jar of blue dye down the back of my leg.

Gentian violet is a beautiful colour and just one of a range of exquisite dyes that, very quickly, turned us into silk addicts. I attended three workshops with Di Teasdale in which we were taught the basics. This was such a lovely art form that, even with only the basic techniques, we were delighted with our results.

Although I explored and enjoyed abstract design I found that I was always happiest when able to combine it with an area of detailed painting. Initially the sheer brilliance of the silk

colours delighted me—it seemed that no one colour clashed with another, and beautiful hues appeared when unlikely colours ran together. The very nature of the silk thread gave a luminosity to each colour. For a time I worked with anti-diffusants in an attempt to control the dyes. While this worked I suddenly realised that I had been trying to turn silk into paper, thus limiting a beautiful medium. Like a number of silk painters I was finding the gutta visually obtrusive; not entirely unattractive, but rather reminiscent of leadlighting. I began to aim at reducing the effect of gutta and tried to turn to advantage the bleeding of one colour into another. I now work by initially using gutta on the white silk only as a highlight. The lightest colour is then applied and partially contained with gutta, gradually working through to the deepest colours using gutta between colours, but trying to avoid a hard line. I rarely completely outline shapes thus giving the dyes freedom to run. This gives a continuity to the design, apart from creating new colour tones.

For me the attraction to fine detail was still evident and I found myself turning to fabric paints after the silk was steamed. 'That's cheating,' came the cry from Di, but as we'd both made a habit of bending art rules she then smiled and generously ignored by transgressions.

A series of macaw parrot photographs intrigued me for weeks as the silk colours so suited the flashy swathe of tail feathers. I happily painted them over and over again. Using fabric paints for facial details, I delighted in the meticulous detailing of eye and beak to give a contrast with the loose stains of feathers falling down the silk.

Happily I explored birds, animals, landscapes and flowers by sweeping the dyes together and then detailing a small area in fabric paint. I discovered the difference in wiping out with methylated spirits as against the softer effect of water wipeout. Having reached what I considered

Spring rhapsody

Macaw parrots

to be the end of my exploration into the techniques of painting on silk all that remained was to get the finished pieces mounted for display. It soon became evident that framing the silk had covered up the edges and had made it difficult to discern that the paintings were on silk.

The next step seemed to me to allow the fabric content of the work to assume more importance. I had always loved the look of the fringe on the few scarves that I had made; this small line of fringeing had a different sheen and delicacy from the main silk piece. I decided to incorporate the fringe into the all-over composition. A series of dragonfly and moth paintings allowed me to do this. Some of the moths I cut out and super-imposed on the background silk and some I sealed with a line of overlocking and pulled the threads to make fringed wings. The chain of overlocking thread made a fragile body for my dragonflies.

I have painted a series of 'this is where I live' pictures with very soft backgrounds, ranging from deserts to rainforests. Having painted the picture I found that by washing water over the entire silk it gave me the muted effect required. Next I painted a small fringed silk strip with a finely detailed subject (flora or fauna) indigenous to the particular landscape and laid it across the background area. Sometimes I chose a different type of silk for the detailed subject, combining a satin over a flimsy gauze. My experiments with padding and machine work came next. These were very simple as I was about as adept with a combine harvester or chain saw as a sewing machine. However the three dimensional effect given by this approach was interesting. I padded small parts of my picture—thereby avoiding the move into the field of fabric craft.

So far I have limited my collages to a variety of silk weights, cut-outs and fringeing—simple combinations. I enjoy painting a silk picture with the emphasis on colour and limited exploration of the fabric.

Left: Mog territory

Below left: I can catch dandelions.

Below: Cats on mats

Above: Oyster shells   *Right: Bush orchid*

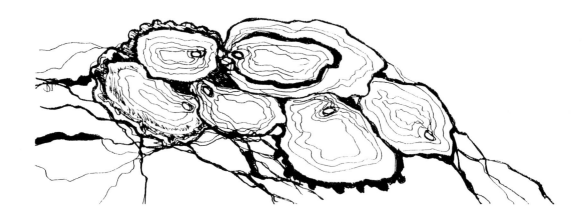

Left: Cats depicted on silk satin   *Top: Silk ensemble with macaw motif*

3

Batik

Ilona Lasmanis

ILONA LASMANIS was born in Germany in 1945. She studied at East Sydney Technical College and has a diploma of Art Education. In 1980–1985 Ilona exhibited in the ACT, Northern Territory and South Australia.

MY INVOLVEMENT with fabric and dyes is an extension of my interest in print making.

Gradually I have supplemented the traditional batik methods with a combination of methods which might include spraying, stamping, printing, dipping and painting the fabric to achieve the effect I want.

I often use Australian motifs for my designs because these images offer so much scope for the use of rich colours and textures.

I think of the clothes and fabrics as wearable pictures.

BATIK is a method of patterning fabric which uses wax as a resist when applying colour. Originally from Indonesia it is now an internationally known technique.

EQUIPMENT

Traditionally a canting is used to apply the wax to the fabric. This consists of a small metal bowl with a spout through which the hot wax is dispensed. The size of the spout controls the width of the wax line. Wax can also be applied by using stamps and paint brushes.

An electric fry pan is commonly used to heat batik wax although commercial heating units are also available. The wax should be hot enough to allow easy flow through the canting. Too high a temperature will burn the wax.

Although some artists have their own recipes, cracking and non-cracking wax is readily available through commercial suppliers. Non-cracking wax

Left: Traditional kimono. This design depicts Japanese women wearing a kimono featuring Australian flora and fauna.

is frequently favoured, particularly when working with fabric to be dyed in a dye bath. This type of wax is more flexible and can withstand the rougher treatment of fabric being handled through a number of dye baths.

A variety of improvised tools can also be used to apply wax to make textures and achieve special effects, for example, sponge, pieces of wood, wire grating, potato masher, tooth brush etc.

THE DESIGN

The main shapes of the design are drawn on the fabric in pencil, charcoal or chalk before the fabric is stretched over the frame. The design lines are then redrawn in wax to make the dam walls which will prevent the dye from spreading to other areas of the design.

If large areas of the design need to be blocked out, a paint brush should be used to apply wax.

STRETCHING THE FABRIC

To apply the wax the fabric is stretched over a frame. A variety of commercial frames are available, however, a simple wooden frame and drawing pins are satisfactory. Care should be taken not to tear the fabric once it is firmly stretched.

DYES

There are a variety of dyes suitable for working on silk. Each dyestuff has its own requirements, recipes and methods of working supplied by the manufacturer or supplier.

When using a dye bath always wear rubber gloves.

When using unknown dyes it is advisable to experiment with some test strips before committing the final piece to an irreversible process.

DYE APPLICATION

To prepare the dyes follow the manufacturer's

instructions. Fabric can be dyed in one piece in a dye bath or individual areas of a design can be hand painted. Frequently a combination of techniques is used which might include dipping, painting and using an airbrush.

FIXING THE DYE

The fixing method will depend on the type of dye used. The instructions are supplied by the manufacturer. Dyes suitable for silk are frequently fixed by steaming although with many dyes fixing agents are available.

REMOVAL OF WAX

If the fabric is to be steamed it is advisable to remove the wax before steaming by ironing the fabric between sheets of clean, absorbent paper and then rinsing the fabric in white spirit.

FURTHER READING

Traditional and Modern Batik. Miep Spee, Kangaroo Press.

The kimonos

The two kimonos were designed as a pair. There are several layers of reference in the design. Since the origin of the kimono is Japan I decided to use a Japanese motif for the design and at the same time I wanted the design to reflect the country in which they were made. I also decided that I wanted to use the traditional kimono design for the garments which meant having a seam through the centre back. This decision was relatively critical in the final assembly of the kimonos because the pieces were painted individually first, so the designs had to match!

My decision to make Australian kimonos provided the opportunity to use Australian flora and fauna as the motifs for my designs.

Reflecting the Japanese origins of the kimono, the first kimono features Japanese women wearing traditional kimonos depicting Australian flora and fauna. One woman wears a kimono of flannel flowers and geckos, another kimono displays frill-necked lizards and the third stylised sulphur-crested cockatoos. This kimono is lined with silk featuring trumpet jasmine and geckos.

The second kimono refers directly to the first, featuring the sulphur-crested cockatoo design realised as an individual kimono. The lining of this kimono shows the cockatoos flying away.

METHOD

Heavy satin silk was used for the kimonos and a light scarf weight silk for the lining.

Drimaraine K fibre reactive dyes were used. These dyes are fixed by Drimafix.

Non-cracking wax was used for the dam lines and to block out large areas.

The dye was applied through painting, even on the larger areas of the kimono. As this can be a bit tricky, care must be taken to get the dye even over the larger areas.

Far left: Kimono lining decorated with trumpet jasmine and gecko lizards

Left: Stylised sulphur crested cockatoos. Interior design depicts their flight.

Above: Kimono interior depicting flight of sulphur crested cockatoos

Cat à la airbrush

4
Airbrushing
Dae and Lucy

*B*OTH *Dae and Lucy have been successfully involved with hobby ceramics, teaching and exhibiting at shows for over 8 years.*

During a get-together they decided it would be nice to try something different using the skills they had to give their students something new. They decided on silk painting.

When translating their designs to silk they found there was not a large range of colours available so they began experimenting with dyes.

Seminars using their product created such a response that they decided it would be nice to have an Australian product on the market. A natural progression was to produce the dyes and market them under their name 'Daluce Silk'.

Lucy and Dae's work is complementary. Lucy excels in flower decoration and Dae in abstract and fantasy designs.

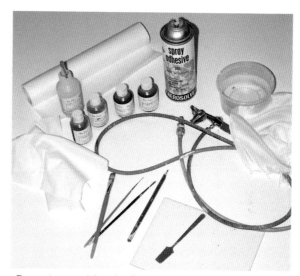

Preparing to airbrush, firstly lay out equipment

THE PRACTICE of airbrushing has long been part of the world of the graphic artist. It is a means by which fantasy, nature and the manmade can be visually rendered with incredible detail and subtlety. Perhaps of all the artforms, the airbrush has the potential to provide the greatest sense of texture and space. Fine examples of skilled airbrushing are before us daily in the form of advertising: billboards, magazines and familiar things such as the labels on soup tins and sauce bottles.

That this is a medium which requires practice, patience and careful planning there is no doubt. There is no doubt also that this is a totally absorbing means of expression for the non-professional in which the investment of time is rewarded with new adventure.

The airbrush is a painting instrument that can produce effects ranging from pencil lines to smooth uniform areas of colour. This does not mean you can throw away your brushes. Your brushes and brush skills will be needed to emphasise and detail your work. For the beginner

the Paasche H series is recommended. It is very important to read the instructions provided with the airbrush. Practise varying the width of the spray to get good control.

We have used the airbrush for speed and ease of colour application giving subtle shading which, using a brush, would take years of practice.

EQUIPMENT
Airbrush
Illustration board or Masonite
Silk for testing colour
Air supply
Tracing paper
Water
Painting media
Brushes
Spray adhesive
Pencil
Pallet
Silk dyes
Tissues or cotton buds
NB All silk dyes used throughout these exercises are Daluce Silk Kolor and are identified by name rather than hue.

Right: Masking the eyes with frisk paper, lightly brush background and cat features with colour.

Far right: Spanish brown deepens background and shadows on cat.

Right below: Painting medium is applied to the eyes and nose. These areas are worked in detailed brushwork.

Trouble shooting for an airbrush

Problem	Cause	Cure
No air flow	Airfeed in airbrush blocked	Remove needle and nozzle, blast air in opposite direction to airfeed while keeping air valve open. Check reservoir for debris.
No colour being sprayed	Reservoir empty	Fill
	Mixture too thick	Empty reservoir and remix
	Mixture dried in nozzle	Remove needle and nozzle and clean
Bubbles appearing in colour cap	Mismatched nozzle and cap	Replace with matched nozzle seat
	Nozzle cap loose	Tighten
Spitting or spatter	Air pressure too low	Check and tighten nut fittings
	Solid particles in nozzle	Remove and clean
	Mixture too thick or badly mixed	Add more solvent or remix
	Worn or damaged nozzle	Replace
Spatter at angle	Needle bent	Repair if possible
	Nozzle damaged	Replace
Spatter at begining of stroke	Build-up in nozzle cap due to closing of air flow before needle seating in nozzle	Ensure needle is seated in nozzle before stopping airflow
	Damaged needle	Repair if possible
	Solid particles in nozzle	Remove and clean
Spatter at end of stroke	Damaged needle or nozzle	Replace
Spidering effect	Airbrush too close to surface	Move it back
	Too much flow	Adjust needle control
	Poor lever control	Practise
Flooding of colour	Mixture over diluted	Remix
	Poor airbrush control	Practise
	Erratic movement of airbrush	practise

The above information was supplied by Jill Bridgeman of Verdun, SA.

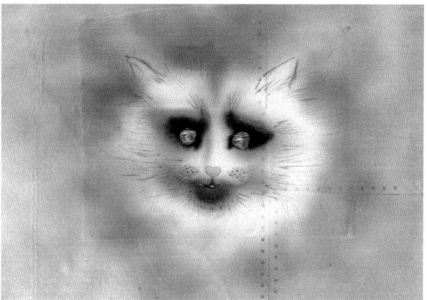

Le chat

Apply adhesive to board.

Choose a subject and draw or trace features onto paper and adhere to board under silk.

Spray traced paper with adhesive.

Carefully put on silk.

Starting at the bottom attach one inch (2.5 cm) of silk and stroke from centre out to the sides two inches (5 cm) at a time.

Mask off eyes with Frisk paper.

Starting off with Butterscotch, lightly airbrush the background around the cat and on features.

Always test your airbrush on scrap fabric before applying to your work.

Changing to Spanish Brown, apply around cat where white areas were left. Deepen features with this colour.

Burnt Sugar is next, again around features. Return to Butterscotch if area looks too purply.

Apply Wallaby Brown, still deepening features.

Use tissue to blot any excess colour beading up on the masked out eyes. Remove Frisk from eyes.

Apply painting medium to nose, eyes and areas that are to be detailed. With colour mixed in your painting medium pull in the fine hairs with a detailing brush.

Then go over some of the hair just with water on the brush.

Fill in the eyes with Butterscotch and Black pupils.

Airbrush over the top part of eyes to soften them.

Mixing a touch of Wallaby Brown into Rocket Red fill in nose.

Put White highlights on eyes with fabric paint.

Below: Airbrush outside edges and tips of plumage
Right: Black deepens shadows on underside of tongue and beak of the flower.

Birds of paradise

Develop a design on backing paper.

Adhere to illustration board.

Spray with spray glue and adhere silk to board—if using banded silk make sure lines are straight.

Airbrush outside edges and tips of plumage with Marigold highlighted with Tangerine.

Complete colour on plumage using Rocket Red, highlight with Scarlet.

Using Burnt Sugar, airbrush stems and beak.

To get sharpness on beak place masking tape either side to form point, taking care not to let the colour run off the tape.

Highlight underside of beak and stems with Avocado.

Mask off tongue to get sharp point.

Airbrush with Glazier Grey.

Using Glazier Grey, shadow stems and underside of beak.

Using Black, deepen shadow on underpart of tongue and beak.

Using brush with water, mottle plumage till desired effect is achieved.

Detail with White fabric paint.

Recommended airbrush for beginners: 'H-series' with 30 PSI using the No. 1 tip.

Far left: Mask flowers prior to commencing lattice work

Left: Subtlety of colour is the hallmark of the airbrush

5
The art of marbling
Wendy Alland

*W*ENDY ALLAND *is an artist who seeks expression through touch, feel and colour, working through the medium of fine fabrics and the traditional art of marbling.*

Inspiraton for Wendy's themes of Opal, Barrier Reef, Harlequin and Outback is taken from Australia's natural wonders and reflects the brilliance of light, the kaleidoscope of colour, the contrasts of climate and the fire of the earth.

Wendy's unique contribution to the marbling artform has been to adapt it to fabric in order to create a wardrobe of wearable art—an original blending of function and self expression.

In the two years since Wendy's art has been commercially available, she has already received recognition through invitations to exhibit nationally and through purchase by the South Australian Art Gallery.

PAPER was marbled in the Orient as early as the eighth century. The process derives its name from the veining of marble. The art of marbling travelled to Persia and Turkey and reached Europe in the late fifteenth century.

Marbling is the transfer of floating colours from the surface of a tray of water thickened with carragheen moss to paper, fabric or leather. Fantasy designs can be created by combing.

It is *impossible* to produce two identical marbled pieces.

Materials for marbling
SIZE
This is a gel-like substance which, when blended with water, creates a solution with a high enough tension to allow floating colours to be drawn. Carragheen moss, a seaweed known also as Irish moss, is commonly used. Use distilled water or rain water for mixing colours and size.

Left: Flight of fantasy by Wendy Alland

Carragheen recipe
In a blender mix 1 tablespoon of carragheen with 300 ml hot water. Blend for 30 seconds. While blades are still running, add 1 litre of cold water and blend for 30 seconds more. Only rain water or distilled water should be used as tap water may contain excessive minerals and, for a beginner, be too difficult to adjust. The resulting size should be a clear amber colour, gelatinous to the touch but liquid. Add 1 teaspoon of dettol to size to prevent algae. Cover and leave in a cool area for at least 12 hours, this will mature the size for best results.

COLOURS
Various paints and inks are available from art shops. Designer's gouache has a high pigment of gum content and gives a strong colour. I always enjoy using it.

DISPERSING AGENT
Ox gall is a fluid, literally the bile of the ox, mixed with colour, which makes the marbling possible by breaking the viscosity (surface tension) of the gelatinous size and allowing the colours to float on the surface of the bath instead of sinking. It forms a microscopic wall of fat around each drop of colour, preserving its identity and allowing colours to be drawn into designs. Since it is added to the colour a drop at a time, a bottle will last for many marbling sessions.

Ox gall is available from suppliers of artists' materials in the section that deals with water colours and designer's gouache, or you may prepare your own as detailed below.

Recipe for ox gall
Fresh and undiluted ox gall obtained from an abattoir can be treated in the following manner: Leave the gall, which will be a thick yellow fluid, until it settles to a clear dark brown. Drain off the clear liquid, add 1 tablespoon of gin to each

pint (600 ml) and then bottle. Store in cool place. Ox gall, like port, improves with age, however, it will always be very bitter smelling.

ALUM (aluminium potassium sulphate)
Before paper or fabric can be marbled it must be treated with alum, a mordant or fixative, so that the transfer from one surface to another can take place.

The fabric must be washed in hot water and some form of stripping powder, rinsed and dried.

When fabric is perfectly dry, wearing rubber gloves soak it in warm alum and hang on the clothes line, taking care not to overlap fabric. Watch for rain which will wash out the solution. Allow to dry and then iron as flat as you can manage, ready to marble.

Depending on the size of paper or fabric you decide to marble, your tray should be about 4–5 cm deep to start. The tray can be made of fibreglass, wood, plastic or metal to whatever size you require. I suggest a small tray for beginners.

Paper must be sponged evenly in a warm alum (but not soaked) and allowed to dry. Keep dry paper in a flat press or with weights on top ready for marbling.

Alum recipe
1 tablespoon of alum to 600 ml of cold water (rainwater or distilled). Wearing rubber gloves melt alum in a saucepan being careful *not to inhale* fumes. If you find the alum solution has crystallised reboil for further use. Store in a glass bottle.

FABRICS
Pure silks such as Habutai or satin are most suitable (fabrics must not have slubs in the weave). Chiffon is very difficult to handle as the fabric shrinks when laid onto the marbling tray.

Cottons with a synthetic mix are very easy to handle and give a high vibrancy and clarity.

Leather, which should be sponged not soaked in alum, is extremely difficult to lay as it is not flat, but cut into smaller pieces it can be managed. Gold and silver inks create amazing effects.

PAPER
Art/craft papers, bond (not flimsy), oriental and hand made papers will all marble, however some papers are coated in a chemical that repels the alum. Buy test sheets before buying larger quantities.

Candles can be fun to marble but only oil colours will adhere to wax.

Conditions for marbling

The perfect conditions for marbling are cool, 10–15°C (50–60°F), humid and clean.

Avoid direct sunlight on papers or tray, as this dries out paper and interferes with the surface tension of the carragheen. Air conditioning and heaters remove too much moisture but you can spray the room with a mist of distilled water or set up a humidifier.

A higher temperature causes the size to have less surface tension (a runnier consistency), which gives less control for marbling patterns but is great for stone and granite designs. Either marble early morning or late evening when the temperature is cooler for more difficult designs such as feather.

The size bath will require daily adjustment and only warm water should be added, never cold, to thin the size to a medium cream consistency. No draughts or dust should be allowed in the vicinity. Dust floating in the room or on the tray is the main cause of spots in marbling.

Preparing to marble

Before floating the colours, skim the size with strips of newspaper and a skimmer board to remove dust particles and break the surface tension so that the inks can float in round 5 cm globules.

Fabric marbling inks are thinned with white spirit to the consistency of runny cream and added in single drops with a bamboo (sate) stick onto the surface of the carragheen solution, aiming for the drops to form 5 cm globules. One or two drops of ox gall per colour are also added. An eye dropper is another way to place colour.

Paper marbling uses the same procedure. To use tube gouache, squeeze approximately 2 teaspoons of colour into a container, adding water sparingly to form a cream consistency.

I would advise floating only a few colours, i.e. 4, so that control is learned. With a needle or comb rake the 5 cm globules of colour through each other creating different effects (similar to icing a cake).

There are a number of traditional marbled patterns based on combing techniques. You can see these in many libraries in their rare book sections.

LAYING FABRIC

Carefully lower the fabric onto the floating colours, leave for half a minute and then gently lift out of the tray, drain, rinse fabric by pouring water over it and allow to dry on lines. When dry, depending on what marbling inks were used (read manufacturer's instructions), iron fabric between paper towels. Paper is not ironed but allowed to dry by pegging and then flattening in a press. The marbling tray surface is skimmed with newspaper and is then ready to use again.

EQUIPMENT CHECK LIST

Straws for blowing colours
Combs of various shapes (an afro creates interesting designs)
Whisk
Eye dropper
Skimmer board
Newspaper
Water near marbling area
Sate sticks
Glass jars for mixing colours
White spirit
Electric blender
Tablespoon
Bucket
Rubber gloves
Spray
Marbling tray
Sponge
Paper towels
Pegs

Problems and Solutions

1. Stars: Indicate skin on surface. *Solution:* skim surface with newspaper, stir and reskim.

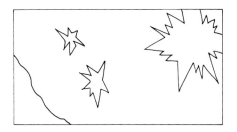

2. Dust: Solution: spray room, close windows, skim tray.

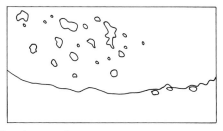

3. Break-up: Solution: colours may not be thoroughly mixed.

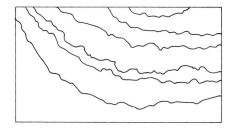

4. Ragged edges: Immature size or warm conditions. *Solution:* leave size for 6 more hours. Marble at coolest time of day.

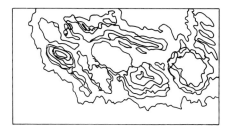

When marbling don't fight against the elements, flow with them, it is less frustrating and more creative.

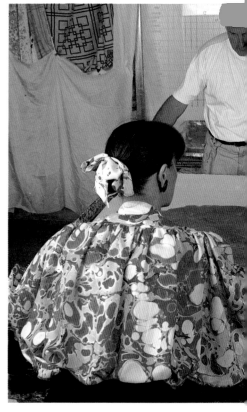

Top: Marbling inks are thinned to the consistency of runny cream and dropped onto the prepared bed.

Above: Strips of newspaper or a skimmer board is used to remove dust particles.

Top: Disturbing the surface of the tray moves the colour and changes the patterns.

Above: Lowering silk onto the floating colour

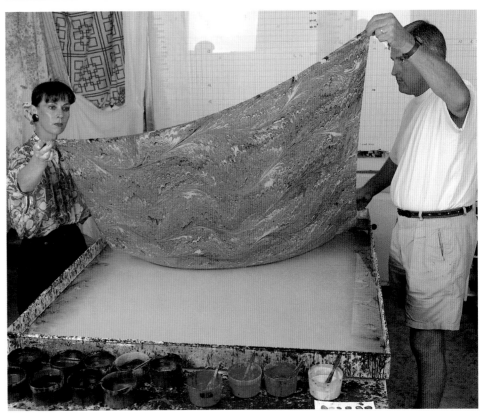

Top: More colour can be added, this displaces the colour underneath.
Above: Half a minute in the tray converts white silk to detailed colour pattern.

6

An introduction to silk painting
Di Teasdale

Materials and equipment

A GLANCE at the index of this book will indicate that the art of silk decoration involves many different techniques and no doubt a variety of materials. The most common form of silk decoration however involves the use of gutta resist and washes of colour. The results usually end up around someone's neck, framed or in a bucket of bleach.

Tooling up for one of the sessions shouldn't involve a huge financial outlay. Many items are to be found around the house. A kitchen can easily be converted to an authentic looking studio, but do cover up with paper and plastic or no-one will eat there again.

Having decided to be really serious about this, these are the articles you will require. Non-household items will be available at most craft outlets in a variety of brands.

Silk, Habutai or Jap
Dye
Gutta
Pipette and application bottle
Gutta solvent
Brushes, several sizes
Drawing pins
Sticky tape
Cotton buds
Salt, several varieties
Alcohol (ethyl rubbing)
Pencils
Tissues or paper towel
Scissors
Hair dryer
Clean jars
Rubber gloves
Frames and stretchers
Optional
Coloured or metallic gutta
Antifusant
Pre-hemmed scarves

A good way to start silk painting is to join a class where materials and tuition are provided. Upon completion the student will either tool up or ship out.

DYE
Prepared commercial dye is most commonly used by hobby painters. This is easily accessible and comes in a wide range of colours thereby eliminating the need to mix colours for those not sure what they're doing. There are many brands available, often imported from France and, more recently, some excellent Australian products have reached the markets. Dye is water based and has a long shelf life. It should be stored out of direct sunlight with lids securely fastened. Each brand has a commercial dilutant which may be purchased for breaking down colour. This is really only necessary if a large area of silk must be very even or the diluted colour is to be stored any length of time. On the whole, the water-based colour responds well to being broken down by rain or distilled water. Some colours once diluted have a tendency to develop slimy sediment, even undiluted colour will congeal with age. Warming the container externally until the colour dissolves will render it usable. Never return diluted colour to the original bottle.

Gloves should be worn when working with dye. An application of barrier cream prior to a painting session helps slow absorption of colour through the skin. The complexities of dye technology are explained in more detail in the chapter 'Dyestuffs and dyeing'.

RESISTS
Silk painting employs several forms of resist. These solutions fill the fibre so that dye-laden liquid cannot pass through. These resists are used to form a pattern or to protect an already coloured area.

Wax

This resist is probably the oldest. For centuries batik paintings have been produced by fine crafts people to decorate woven cloth.

Gutta

This is a clear latex solution which is applied to silk to isolate areas of design that are to be coloured. Gutta may be coloured with colourant or purchased in black, gold and silver; it is most often used in its clear form.

The method of application can vary. Most commonly used is a soft plastic bottle with a nozzle top on which a plume or pipette has been secured. Small acetate cones not unlike an icing bag are sometimes used.

Whatever the tool, the most important thing is the quality of line. Broken lines mean leaking colour which spreads into other areas. When this happens dry the silk, repair the line, repeat colour and hope for the best. Gutta can be removed by soaking in white spirit or turpentine but this is not recommended until colour fixing is complete. Therefore, if your applicator bottle cannot draw properly improvise or start again.

Coloured gutta can produce lovely results. But articles should be clearly marked 'Do not dry clean' for obvious reasons.

Water-based Gutta

This form of gutta is produced from vegetable gum. It is often applied to larger areas of textile designs. Its edges are less crisp depending on the strength of the mixture. This often produces a result not unlike a torn edge which can be particularly pleasing.

Modern technology is working hard to develop a water-based gutta that will produce fine strong lines. This, no doubt, is just a matter of time.

PIPETTE OR PLUME

This is a metal nib to fit the gutta bottle. Nibs come in various sizes, No. 6–7 being the most common size used.

BRUSHES

A variety of sizes is useful. Ideally brushes should carry a quantity of liquid and retain a good point as for water colour painting.

Except for frames (see below), basic kits really only require dyes, brushes, gutta applicator and silk. However, the following items are an inexpensive addition to the box which allow great diversity in painting styles.

DIFFUSER

This is an agent which, when added to dye, causes the colour to bleed more freely. Lovely in soft backgrounds, also in isolated areas of intense colour when several colours are used.

ANTIFUSANT

Also known as painting medium, this is a substance which inhibits the dye's ability to migrate along the silk thread. As well, this resist can be painted upon. Antifusant can be used in several ways. It can be painted directly onto the silk where required. Once dry this area will be quite stiff and behave more like paper than silk as a painting surface. Liquid colour placed around these areas will run to the edge of the treated surface then stop. This often leaves a slightly uneven line not unlike an edge of torn paper. Another use for antifusant is to colour it and apply to an area. This technique is often used to detail nearly completed pieces—stamens on flowers, whiskers on possums etc.

FRAMES AND STRETCHERS

Silk is by nature soft and slippery and impossible to paint unless it is stretched.

Frames or stretchers can be as simple as an

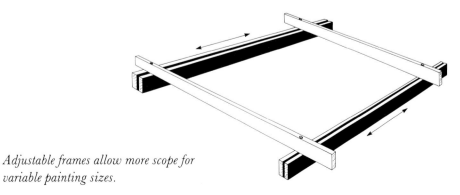

Adjustable frames allow more scope for variable painting sizes.

Above: Materials for a silk painting session many of which are household items

Right: Stretchers in a variety of shapes suited to scarves

Below right: Adjustable stretchers are best. If not, choose several sizes which have a comfortable format.

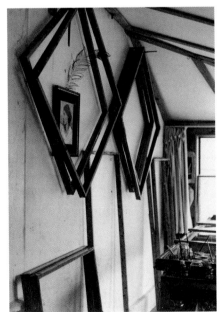

old picture frame. All that is needed is four wooden edges to which silk can be taped or pinned.

Ideally an adjustable frame is best, allowing freedom in the size and shape of the painting while maintaining tension from each direction. Most handymen just love the prospect of making these and hurl themselves into the project with gay abandon, usually resulting in dozens of variations and several editions, each better than the last.

Stretching the silk

Pin one side with drawing pins or staples. Pin the opposite side next, then the other two sides until there is an even tension throughout. Once the silk becomes damp it will sag—more tension can then be applied.

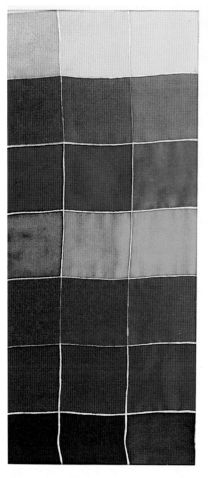

E

A B C D

Repeated use of the frame results in colour being absorbed by the wood. Masking tape can be used to cover the edges and eliminate the introduction of unwanted colour.

First Projects

Getting to know the properties of silk can be an exciting experience. It can also be a little frightening. Start with something simple and don't be afraid to waste some silk.

Dye is water based and the silk is absorbent not unlike water colour paper in fact. Here are some simple experiments which will help you understand the character of this medium.

Firstly, stretch some scrap silk and fill the brush with colour. Take care to shake off the excess liquid. Run the brush across the silk and watch the colour spread. Run another brush load, perhaps another colour, across the silk about 1 cm (½″) below the previous line. Repeat; watch the dye-laden liquids compete for surface space, one against the other, the larger wetness overrunning less wet areas.

Solid plain areas of colour are produced in a

Colour chart (left)
Left line: Two applications of colour
Middle line: One application of colour
Right line: Colour diluted 100% with water

Bottom: Multi media design produced with gold, silver and black gutta. Antifusant was used on the leaves with no hard outline.

Top: (A) hard line softened on one side with water
(B) Colour mixed with antifusant produces a dry non-spreading quality.
(C) Colour applied to a wet surface
(D) Water has been wiped along either side of the coloured line resulting in feathery edges.
(E) Salt applied to an area of moist colour

similar manner placing the lines closer together, working quickly with a large brush.

For the second exercise take a clean brush and lightly wet the silk surface. Run colour across this area as above. The colour will spread slowly leaving soft fuzzy edges.

Now run a colour-laden brush across the dry surface. Take a water-laden brush and run it along one side of this line. The results will be a hard line on one side and a soft line on the other. Water marks or hard edges can be softened by this method. Playing with the colour in this method is not a waste of time. Watching colour migration and the habits of overlapping colours, water marks and liquids displacing liquids is valuable experience.

During this introduction to the medium there is fun to be had and some lovely effects to achieve using simple methods.

SALT—A MAGIC TEXTURE

This is a fun technique which can be used to add interest to colour or texture to an area, i.e. textured border to a scarf. Materials required: clean water, colours and a variety of salt. Table salt, coarse salt, rock salt; I even have some which has sheep and kangaroo droppings in it, collected from a salt pan, courtesy of a friend. I haven't quite managed to use this batch up yet. Pickling salt is also good and available from your local butcher for a small fee. The salt should be dried and stored in airtight jars since it is hygroscopic and becomes quite damp in humid and wet weather conditions.

Method

Stretch silk, apply colour so that the surface is wet but not running into pools. Sprinkle with salt. Like magic the salt soaks up the colour while it continues to migrate along the thread. The result is fascinating. Patterns reminiscent of coral, sometimes swirling lines or lovely textures are left on the silk as it dries.

Dust off the salt once the silk is dry and steam with butcher's paper between each layer of fabric. This is a good technique for a beginner to play with because right from the start usable scarves can be produced. Experiment with different colour combinations. Leave some areas white and wash others with water. There is only one word of warning. Should the result be disappointing *don't* work back over the top. The result is a mess; better to rinse out silk, iron dry and try again.

I love this particular technique and frequently use it for texture behind a design.

HALOING

As the word suggests this method produces a spreading hole in solid colour. Methylated spirit or rubbing alcohol is touched onto a coloured surface. The colour disperses softly leaving a ring around the outside. When worked onto a wet surface in close spots, the spreading shapes compete for space and distort interestingly.

INLAY PAINTING TECHNIQUE

This method uses gutta to draw a design onto the silk. The line of latex solution penetrates the fibres and forms a block to the flow of dye. This enables a design to be established with distinct areas of colour separated by a white line. A drawing quality can be developed in a design with softened lines of detailing as in the iris study.

Controlling the gutta is a skill in itself. Practise on scrap silk. Place the nib against the silk, resting not pressing. Squeeze the bottle gently and move it across the silk when the gutta begins to flow. At first this action will be in fits and blurts. Try to perfect an even thickness of line; make boxes and rings to fill with colour taking care no breaks in the lines occur. Quality of line is important for two reasons. Artistically even lines look better, particularly when working with coloured gutta. The other reason is that even lines are not likely to have breaks in them and will result in less bleeding of colour from one area to another. Should this occur, dry and recoat with gutta to seal thoroughly.

It is a good idea, about this time, to make a swatch of all your colours. Draw up a grid allowing for three spaces per colour. Apply two coats in the first one, one coat in the next and a 100% dilution of colour in the third. This reference will be used often when working out what colours suit each other. As more colours are purchased these can be added to the swatch.

BLENDING COLOURS

Large areas and background are easily blended by the following method. You will need a rubber glove, cotton wool or scraps of clean silk.

Select several complementary colours which should be mixed and close at hand. It will be necessary to work quickly before the colours dry.

Apply colour in a swirling movement with a small dye-laden cloth. Apply one colour after another, close but not touching. Take a water-laden cotton wool ball and run through the uncoloured areas to soften edges.

Don't be tempted to play. Should the silk develop soggy muddy patches, use a dry cotton ball or tissue to mop up excess liquid. The fabric appears quite different once it has dried. If the results of your labour are unexciting, consider drawing an all-over design with gutta. Pay particular attention to the areas of better colour.

Select a strong complementary colour and coat the entire surface. The gutta resist will feature the pleasing colour in the form of the design and the background colour will diminish the muddy patches. These pieces are excellent for quilting and make lovely jackets and vests.

SHADING A DESIGN

Shading techniques are used to add interest to the focal point of painting. This method provides relief from the flat coloured-in effect while still maintaining an overall colour.

Once the gutta drawing is complete take a small amount of colour and apply this to an area, for example a leaf. Place green at the base of the leaf, then taking a clean water-laden brush place a drop at the tip of the leaf. The green dye will be drawn towards the tip of the leaf. This produces a three dimensional look ideal for curving flat shapes. This simple method can be used most effectively using several colours, achieving an over-all effect of green on a leaf but including the interest of a variety of colours and tones.

Troubleshooting for Silk Painting

Problem	*Cause*	*Cure*
Gutta		
Gutta line allows colour to bleed through	Uneven pressure when applying gutta	Practise easy strokes and boxes to perfect pressure
	Pressing too heavily on silk—this produces a thin line	As above
	Gutta too thick	Dilute with commercial thinner appropriate to brand of gutta
	Gutta drying too quickly. The fibre is not saturated.	Dilute if thick. Extreme heat will produce this result — work in cooler weather
	Not enough care taken to seal joins in design	Always pay attention to joins to produce a secure dam
Dye-related problems		
Colour passes through gutta line	Broken line	Dry silk, repair line Brush with water if on white silk Draw something else next to bleed, colour both areas Alcohol may be applied with a cotton bud to bleach the patch although often a stain remains. Improvise.
Colour streaky	Over-diluted dye	Colour may be diluted with rain or distilled water. For evenness and longevity it should be diluted with a commercial dilutant
	Not applied evenly	Practise even overlaying of strokes to produce block colour
	Colour applied over a dry area	Always work wet for even colour. When repairing recoat entire area

The iris has been drawn directly onto the silk with clear gutta. Colour has been applied to produce light shading; a partial wash has been applied to background.

Highlights have been developed on the flower by use of a clean water-laden brush. More depth has been added to the area behind the iris.

By the use of an additional wash, other colours and greater depth have been developed in the painting. The background has received an all-over wash with several colours.

Depth and final detail have been added to both flower and background by painting directly onto the silk with darker colours.

A wash of pale colour was laid down prior to commencing this study. The painting was produced by the above method but the end result is softer.

This iris was painted with a mixture of antifusant and dye applied directly to the silk surface.

	Size in fabric	Size is sometimes used to give bulk to fabric. This gums the fibres. If in doubt test for this by diluting iodine with water. Apply to small area of silk. If size is present the silk will turn pale mauve
Stored colour has sludge in jar	Diluted colour can be contaminated from the air and dirty brushes	Heat colour in microwave or stand jar in warm water. Colour may be strained through gauze or pantyhose
	Diluted colour has been returned to neat dye jar	As above and use quickly
Colour has congealed	Age	Heat gently
Colour jumps the line at the edge of the silk	Torn silk has small threads which will transport colour around a gutta line	Apply gutta to edge of silk then form a 'T' along the silk edge

Miscellaneous problems

Salt technique not working	Silk too wet	Dry, rinse, try again.
	Silk too dry	As above. Salt either works or doesn't work
	Colour too diluted	Some colours work better than others, experiment
	Salt damp	Dry salt in oven or microwave. Store in air-tight jar
Scarves have dark smudges on the edge	Frames have been used before. Colour creeps out of pin holes	Retape frequently. Wash frames after each use.

Fixing a painting

There are several methods by which a painting may be fixed. By far the best method of fixing is by steaming; the colour is most vibrant and the natural lustre of the silk is restored. However, not everyone has access to a steamer. The following methods of fixing work well but reduce the colour slightly.

AIR CURING

Silk may be left to stand for 48 hours or more to set. This is not recommended for clothing but is fine when a painting is to be framed.

FIXING BATHS

This is basically a process of neutralising the dye. The actual chemical varies depending on the acid or alkaline content of the dye. Always use fixative produced specifically for the dye and follow the instructions on the label. This process should only be undertaken after air curing for at least 48 hours. Actual quantities of fixative to water will vary depending on the brand.

Method

Firstly find a plastic container which is large enough to immerse silk without crushing it. Approximately 4 litres of liquid per 115 × 115 cm silk.

Place silk in bath and agitate from time to time. Folds and creases result in uneven fixing so frequent agitation is important. Continue this process for at least five minutes.

The silk is now permanently fixed. Some colour will have come away in the bath, and all that remains to be done is to wash out chemicals and excess dye. Hand wash until water is clear.

The bath may be re-used while still clean. Pour back into a container through a coffee filter to remove dye particles. Store in a dark place in an airtight container.

Fix light colours first if intending to re-use.

STEAMING

For the best possible results and the most permanent finish steaming is recommended.

This method suspends the silk over a quantity of water which is maintained at a simmer. The moist, hot steam penetrates the layers of silk. The fibres expand and absorb the dyes which, once cooled, are permanently set.

Stainless steel commercial steamers are readily available from most silk outlets. Often these places have a steaming service where your silk can be steamed for a nominal fee.

For the hobby painter who is not trying to paint dress lengths, the average kitchen offers reasonable alternatives. A pressure cooker works well, also any large boiler pot or stewing pan provided it has a fitting lid.

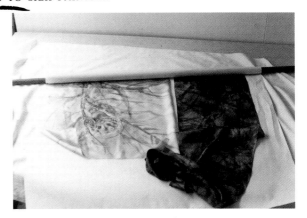

Rolling the silk between layers of butcher's paper

Preparation for steaming

This varies dependent on the type of painting. Silk that has had dyes only applied to it may simply be rolled over a wooden rod or, for the stewpan, on a cardboard cylinder. Care should be taken not to have folds or creases—these become permanent pleats and will not press out.

Silk that has had gutta used in the painting process should be rolled with clean butcher's paper between. Gutta will soften with the heat and can transfer to another layer, better safe than sorry!

Lastly, wrap the whole bundle in the equivalent of a full newspaper; tape securely. The ends of the roll should be open to allow moist air to pass through.

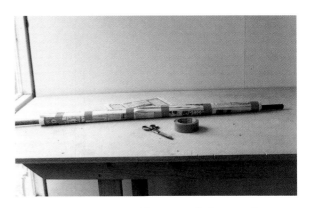

Silk wrapped securely with tape ready for steaming

Steaming times

Small length—1 hour
Large length, 10 metres or more—2 hours
Thick fabric such as satin or corduroy—at least 2 hours.

Improvising a steamer: No. 1

To assemble a steamer some sort of platform should be placed in the bottom of a cooking container with a fitting lid so that the parcel of silk will not become wet. A cake rack or rolled wire works well providing the platform clears the water.

Place the silk package on the rack and cover with a piece of foil. *Do not seal.* The foil is to stop the condensation which forms on the inside of the lid from falling onto the silk package and soaking it. The steam must be allowed to pass around the silk but actual contact with water will spoil the steaming.

Don't be put off by this risk; very little practice is needed to produce perfect steaming and the results are certainly worth the effort.

Silk roll suspended over water in steamer. Small stove being used for heating.

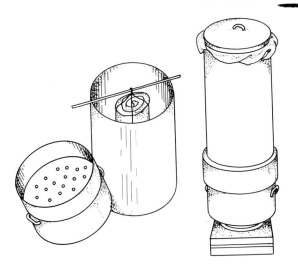

Improvised steam chimney

Basic steamer improvised from a stewing saucepan

Improvising a steamer: No. 2

Take a large deep saucepan like that shown in the diagram, and a cake tin of a matching diameter with sides about 10 cm in height. Punch enough holes in the bottom of the tin to ensure a free flow of steam.

At your local hardware store you should be able to find some lightweight galvanised tubing of a matching diameter so that it will fit snugly into the cake tin, as in the diagram. If this is unavailable, buy a sheet of aluminium and shape it to fit the cake tin. Fasten the edges of the aluminium sheeting together, where it overlaps, with rivets or other metal fasteners. Seal the seams with waterproof tape. You now have what is commonly referred to as a 'bullet steamer'. And you can customise it to suit the width of the fabric you have painted.

The best source of heat is a portable heating element which you can place on the floor.

The fabric to be steamed can be hung from a horizontal support at the top of the chimney or wrapped around a tube, layering the fabric with paper to prevent cross-colouration. Take care that your parcel does not touch the sides.

Fit your steamer, i.e. cake tin and chimney, into the top of the saucepan, now filled with boiling water; cover the top with a thick towel to prevent condensation running back down through your work, put on the saucepan lid and steam as normal.

It is a good idea to use as wide a saucepan as you can find as this will increase the stability of your steamer. Avoid using this sort of steamer in traffic areas where it might be knocked over.

Removing resist

Once a painting is made permanent by bath or steam, the process should be completed by removing unwanted substances.

GUTTA BASED DESIGNS

If the silk is intended for clothing the gutta is best removed. This rubbery solution will stick to the iron and inhibit the soft flow of the silk. Soak the silk in turpentine or white spirits for a while, then gently rub the resisted areas together. Squeeze out several times. Allow to dry completely before continuing with the washing process.

WASHING NEWLY PAINTED SILK

All hand painted silk, regardless of how it is fixed, will retain residual colour that has not been absorbed by the fibre. For the first few washes the excess colour will come away. This doesn't mean that if the silk is constantly washed the colour will fade, merely that more colour was used than was necessary.

Wash in warm soapy water, preferably using a commercial silk wash. Do not leave to soak. Keep the silk moving. Colour will come away, but this is to be expected—it is excess dye. Rinse repeatedly in cold water until it is clear. Drip dry and when almost dry iron with a warm to hot iron.

Caring for silk fabrics

TO WASH OR NOT TO WASH?

This would be the most commonly asked question about silk fabrics. The good news is that *most silks are washable*.

In fact, most silks are better washed than treated with the modern chemicals they are subjected to during dry cleaning.

There are a number of things that the silk fibre does not like and amongst these are many of the detergents available on supermarket shelves. The silk fibre is attacked by alkalis and chlorine bleaches. It is a protein fibre and so when subjected to protein-destroying detergents (the ones containing enzymes) it is severely damaged.

In Australia the reason that most manufacturers, retailers and wholesalers put 'dry clean only' labels on silk garments and fabrics is due to protective consumer laws. This labelling is more a response to the risk of legal damages than a reflection of the true character of the fabric. It can therefore actually be misleading.

If you have any doubts as to whether you can wash a particular garment, either contact the manufacturer or retailer for their advice, or test the fabric for tolerance to water or colour-loss in an inconspicuous area.

There are times when it is appropriate to dry clean a garment and not to wash it. This can apply when certain treatments or finishes have been given to the fabric or garment. The colouring on sequins is often carried on a gelatine base thus the colour would be removed by immersion in water, gelatine being soluble in water. Braiding can very often be coloured with a dye that is fugitive in water and the results of immersion could be disastrous. In addition, the sizing used to stiffen a fabric is often water soluble and washing would result in a limper fabric than the one you started with.

Washing silk is actually very easy:

1. Always *hand-wash* silk in *cold water*.
2. Use a gentle non-detergent cleanser such as Sericare.
3. After washing *spin-dry* using the spin-dry cycle found in most washing machines. Contrary to popular belief this will not damage silk.
4. *Rinse* your garment in *clean cold water*.
5. *After rinsing spin-dry* your garment again to remove the excess water.
6. Place the garment on a hanger (or similar) and allow it to *air-dry* in the *shade*.

7. When the garment is dry or when you wish to wear it iron it with a *warm iron*.

If you do have a silk garment that can only be dry cleaned it is recommended that you ask your dry cleaner to use white spirits as this solution is less harmful to the fibre than some of the other chemicals used.

Above: More colour is applied to background and foreground. Depth is added last with a liner brush.

Left top: The design of the waratah is drawn onto the silk in a light wash of bold colour.

Left bottom: The background is blocked in and depth is developed prior to drawing in detail with clear gutta.

Waratah

These glorious flowers grow prolifically throughout mountainous areas of New South Wales and in particular on the escarpment of the South Coast. Having lived in Wollongong for years I had many opportunities to bush walk through this beautiful area, and witnessing these incredible blooms in their natural environment is something I will always treasure.

As a subject to paint however, their characteristic shapes are unyielding and angular. Their leaves and petals are stiff and waxy. In short, not an easy subject to subdue into graceful composition. Harder still to represent the vibrance of this flower's incredible colour.

This painting has been developed in stages. Firstly a coloured wash of rough shapes was laid down to suggest the composition. Clear gutta was used extensively throughout to establish flower shapes and detail leaves and stems.

Once the gutta was in place attention could be paid to the shading of the main design. Colour was washed across the background in warm and cool shades, intensifying the depth behind the design. Water was used to wipe highlights in the flower petals and darker colour was applied to shadows in both leaves and flowers. Shadow shapes were painted directly onto the background. Final detail was drawn in with black gutta to complete the study.

Sugar glider

Wide ranging phalangers living in coastal forests throughout Australia, these appealing creatures have kite-like membranes which enable them to glide great distances.

This painting has been produced by a combination of methods.

Antifusant was used, as well as clear and black gutta. The painting also required a lot of direct brushwork. The subject was sketched onto the silk in reasonable detail taking care to define areas of highlight and shadow, particularly on the animal. Antifusant was then applied to cover the drawing. Care was taken to create crisp edges by stopping short of the drawn line, so preventing antifusant from spreading beyond the line. Once this was dry the animal was treated to light washes of colour depicting tonal variations of the possum coat. This provides a basis for later fine-line detailing of the fur. Depth was washed into shadow areas and eyes lightly described. Background colour was lightly brushed around the animal taking care not to take a really wet brush too near the antifused area. Soggy backgrounds

can spread, destroying the resisted line. Should this begin to occur use a hair dryer to dry and then recoat with antifusant. For this reason the first background coat should be light in colour and built up in subsequent washes once the subject's outline is clearly established.

Branches and twigs were sketched in by applying colour with a good sable brush. Once dry, clear gutta was used to detail these. The possum received time-consuming detail. Fine hair was painted with small brushes directly onto the antifused area until I felt the creature was nearly complete.

The background was washed with deeper colours and golden highlights added to depict the back-lighting of a nocturnal sky. Shadow forms were painted directly onto the background to produce depth of field.

Black gutta was used to detail foreground branches and twigs. The final touches were applied with a fine brush and a mixture of antifusant and dye. This produced the fine strong lines required to complete the detail of the sugar glider.

Brush-tailed possums

These Australian natives are common throughout the bush, and also renowned for romping around suburban rooftops. The creatures make a delightful subject to paint.

The subject was sketched onto the silk with reasonable detail. Pencil works well on silk provided the silk is stretched sufficiently tightly not to give. Black gutta was then used to draw the detail of the animals and sketch branches etc. Clear gutta was used to draw the gum blossom and also to highlight eyes and whiskers. Light washes of colour were applied to the background and animals. The flowers were treated with bright colour which was later subdued with shading. Depth was added to produce the third dimension and shadow forms were painted directly onto the silk background.

This painting is meant to be a coloured sketch and to convey a feeling of airiness.

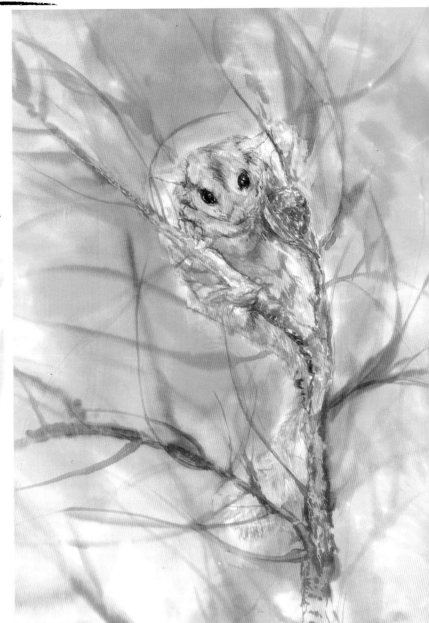

Left: Brush tailed possums depicted on silk in a style not unlike pen and wash

Above left: Stage one of sugar glider colour lightly sketched over antifused area

Above: Background and foreground washes introduce greater depth of field.

Left: Black gutta was used to draw the detail needed to complete the sugar glider.

7
Quilting a jacket
Gaye Liparts

G AYE *was born in New Zealand. She has lived in Australia for three years and considers herself an Australian Kiwi. Her love of quilting, and working with silk developed naturally from her interest in fabric, sewing and art. Relief work in a women's shelter balances the sedentary nature of her quilting interest and university studies.*

FOR MANY traditional quilters machine quilting is seen as quick, easy and second rate; as in all traditional crafts, the contemporary fights for justification and acceptance. Machine quilting, fast in comparison to hand quilting, still requires skill and patience and is never second rate. Moreover, in the world of wearable art where durability and economy count, machine quilting is accepted as practical and preferable.

Until I met Di in 1988 the majority of my quilting was with garment leather, in many ways fun to work with, but restrictive. The possibilities of silk have provided endless surprises. No matter what it is I wish to achieve with silk, adequate thought and forward planning invariably find a way. In this chapter we take a lightweight summer fabric (silk), quilt to provide volume and warmth, then make the resulting cloth into a jacket. This sounds simple I know, and indeed there should be no great difficulties: a certain amount of forethought, some guidance from an experienced quilter, and a little practice in machine skills should eliminate any problems.

The technique I use for quilting hand painted silk is called 'outline' quilting: it enhances the work of the artist, while avoiding obliterating it with stitching lines. When quilting a pictorial scene, i.e. trees and cottage, I work on the principle 'a little goes a long way'. Having said this, an under-quilted jacket looks precisely what it is, under quilted. The trick is to use the eye and apply line to develop a three-dimensional effect, producing the volume required. In all-over patterns, i.e. opal or leaf paintings, the technique

Quilt dominant design lines to complement and strengthen the design

I use creates a flatter look and therefore less volume. With these paintings I tend to quilt approximately 80% of all gutta lines which detracts from the perceived volume but still works, simply because the colour and all-over pattern of the paintings have provided the warmth. When I speak of warmth this is not an illusion, the dacron wadding used as the quilting medium provides more than sufficient warmth. In cooler regions, should more insulation be required, a pure wool wadding is now available.

If you have never made a jacket before, this project is not beyond you. However, it is a good idea, once you have chosen your pattern, to make a 'calico'. This simply requires the construction of the jacket of your choice from a firm fabric (usually calico) to check for suitability of style, fit and any hidden construction problems. Adjust the calico to fit correctly and alter the pattern to match the calico. Although this may seem a long and time-consuming process, it is infinitely preferable to spending long hours quilting and making your silk jacket only to find it is not a good fit. Especially as quilted silk is not easy to reconstruct.

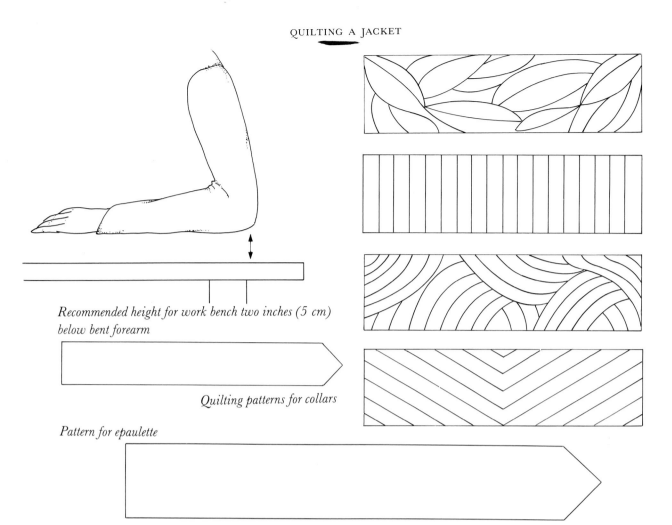

Recommended height for work bench two inches (5 cm) below bent forearm

Quilting patterns for collars

Pattern for epaulette

Elastic casing for jacket bands. Top-stitching produces a more professional finish.

Each section of this chapter advises on different aspects of the jacket. You should read the complete chapter before going ahead with either painting your silk or purchasing a pre-painted length.

For me quilting painted silk is exciting, no matter what the quality of the silk or the talent of the artist. Quilting is an art form in itself, so allow yourself freedom of expression. Read the painting, absorb it, then set about adding the finishing touches to the masterpiece.

Basics first

SEWING MACHINES

Sewing machines, like all machinery, require cleaning, oiling, servicing and adjustments. Incorrect tension, wrong needles, dust on the bobbin case and lack of oil lead to frustration with the work in hand and inevitably another unfinished project for the already overflowing cupboard. Domestic sewing machines should, if used on a reasonably regular basis, be serviced by a qualified mechanic at twelve monthly intervals. Home maintenance should be limited to cleaning, oiling and needle changing with every four hours of sewing time.

Machine manuals

These booklets which arrive with your machine are there for a reason. How many of us have at some stage glanced through one of them then filed it away to be forgotten. Your manual is really your only resource for the use of the machine. Ninety per cent of all problems can be diagnosed and corrected using your manual. Information regarding tension settings and the needle and thread guidance charts are there for that particular

Above: Completed jacket—light, warm and functional

Above left: Silk fabric painted to suit jacket pattern

Left: Back view of completed jacket showing strong definition of tree design

Quilters stitch length of 8–10 stitches to the inch is best.

make and model and should be followed for correct tension control. The troubleshooting section, usually found at the rear of your manual, provides excellent guidelines for correcting tension and stitch formation problems. It is a good idea to store your manual with your machine, or at least readily available; but whatever you do, don't file it away for posterity.

Tension

All machines have their own peculiarities. Check your instruction manual, this will give you the correct guidelines within which to work.

Needles

For silk I use a fine sharp needle size 70/10. *Note:* The maximum number of sewing hours you can expect from your machine needle is four but it is important to change your needle should the slightest burr (blunting) occur. Damaged needles alter tension and stitch formation, causing stitch pull and may even cause fabric damage. It is not uncommon for new needles to be damaged before use. All new machine needles should be checked for burrs before being inserted into the machine. Sewing over pins is probably the most common cause of needle damage, so change the needle immediately if this should happen; and if you are a hoarder of used needles break the habit, throw them away.

Stitch length

For quilting silk, a stitch length of 8–10 stitches per inch allows for flat quilting without pull or stress. Your manual will give you the guidelines for the stitch dial number to achieve this.

Thread

Use a fine polyester thread of good quality as this is what most modern domestic machines and needles are designed for. It is also important to use the same thread in both upper and lower tensions.

THE WORK AREA

A comfortable, well lit work room is, of course, a bonus not readily available to all, and should this be the case then perhaps taking over the dining-room for the duration is a thought. Whatever your circumstances, for a project of this size you will need a reasonable area within which to work—laying out, cutting, quilting, cutting again, pressing and construction, all of which take space, time and thought. Such mundane matters as meals, laundry and general household chores need, to be relegated to out of sight, out of mind and the uncluttered grey matter left for the idiosyncrasies of the project in hand.

Your work area needs to be well lit and have good ventilation, as we will be using spray adhesives. Provide yourself with adequate space for your ironing board, preparation area and sewing machine. To make the most of your time, an undisturbed work area on which you are able to close the door provides the best environment.

A large, firm work surface is necessary. If nothing else is available the kitchen floor can always be a last resort. There are, however, other alternatives. A cutting board, available from retail outlets, usually those that specialise in knit fabrics, can be used to protect a dining room table, on the floor or laid over a bed. The most practical alternative to a specialised cutting/work table is to purchase a length of chip/particle board from your local timber merchant; a measurement of 6′ × 6′ (1.8 m × 1.8 m) sits easily over a double bed and allows a more than adequate area for working with fabrics 115 cm or wider. If you have your own work room, the best solution is a cutting/work table made to measure. The figures quoted above for chipboard are recommended. However, as this is not always practical for a free-standing table, 1.8 × 1.0 m is a functional alternative. The recommended height is individ-ually assessed by measuring the distance from the forearm, bent vertically at the elbow, to the floor, deducting two inches; this gives the best work height for comfort and avoiding back strain.

SCISSORS

Scissors are very much a matter of individual preference, but whatever the choice, one large and one medium pair, well sharpened, with small scissors or thread snips are the basic requirements. When purchasing scissors one needs to bear future use in mind. Ice tempered scissors, although initially more expensive, will give many years of service and are easily resharpened.

Before starting this project prepare suitable work area. Collect sewing materials such as sharp scissors, pins etc. Clean surfaces and set up access to ironing

PINS

The large coloured, glass-headed variety are the better choice when working with wadding for quilting. It is however advisable to remove the white-topped pins before going anywhere near your wadding as they lose themselves in the dacron. A small magnet in the work area is also a good idea; this saves a lot of hunting for lost pins and testy remarks from other members of the family.

WEIGHTS

These provide a useful alternative to pins, especially when cutting. They are placed at intervals across the fabric to hold it secure. I purchase my own from my local fish tackle suppliers and find the 2 oz size most suitable.

SPRAY ADHESIVE

Those suitable for fabric use are now available from most fabric retailers. If purchasing from a hardware shop, be sure to check the label for fabric compatibility.

SLEEVE ROLL

Used for pressing sleeves without creating the pressed seams usually found in jackets, a sleeve roll is easily made by rolling a magazine and taping it tightly, then covering with calico. Suitable measurements for a sleeve roll are 19 cm circumference and 36 cm in length.

POINT PRESSER

This is used for pressing sharp corners, collars etc. My own point pressers are made for me by a friendly handyman, however your nearest tailor may be able to advise. Measurements are:

base	25 × 8 cm	
stand at base	18 cm	
at top	14 cm	
depth	8 cm	

Other equipment requirements: magic tape, tape measure, a clean iron and ironing board.

Materials for the jacket

THE PATTERN

Choose a pattern with uncluttered lines, allowing the painting and quilting of the fabric to provide the focal point. Notched collars and extended shoulder lines work best. Pockets are better kept to the side; zippered, button or stud (snap fastener) closures are all suitable. Leather bands and cuffs, or elastic casings and epaulettes can provide finishing touches without clutter. All commercial pattern ranges provide a good selection from which to choose.

FABRIC

The painted silk for the jacket *must not* be painted to the pattern size but should allow at least 5 cm

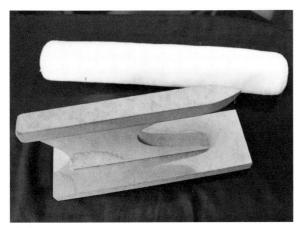

Point presser used to press sharp corners. These are easily made by the family handyman.

Sleeve roll. This is easily improvised from a rolled magazine covered in calico.

(2″) margin around all edges. From the jacket fabric you also require pockets and facings, which should provide continuity of the jacket's main colour. The lining may be painted to the pattern's fabric requirements. Lightweight iron-on interfacing will also be required.

WADDING

85 gm dacron wadding is an easy fibre with which to work; it provides warmth and is a good quilting medium.

THREAD

A good quality polyester thread is required. Choose a colour that will blend into the pattern. Except when working on dark colours I find a light grey colour nearly always suits best.

SHOULDER PADS

Follow the guidelines given on your pattern packet but remember, bone structure normally dictates the type of shoulder pad required. If you find yourself in difficulties try a medium-large raglan shoulder pad as these camouflage problem areas and provide a well defined shoulder line. A 30 cm (12″) length of cotton tape is required if you wish to insert your shoulder pads by machine.

Leather
If using leather for cuffs and lower band, choose a soft garment leather.

Elastic
Elastic for sleeves and lower casing should be 2.5 cm (1″) wide and of the non-roll variety.

Studs (snap fastenings)
Available with suitable applicators from all fabric retail outlets.

Buttons
Follow pattern guidelines.

Starting the jacket

PREPARING THE PATTERN
- Check your body measurements, bust and hip, also finished sleeve and body lengths. Alter pattern as necessary.
- If your painting is pictorial, i.e. a tree scene, pattern placement is extremely important, so drafting an extra front and sleeve pattern piece is advisable, also an extended back pattern piece, as you will be cutting your jacket in a single fabric layer.

- Have all pattern pieces prepared for use but *do not* cut fabric to pattern at this time.

CUTTING
'Measure twice, cut once.'
- The initial cutting of the jacket fabric, apart from pockets and facings, is done without shaping, no necklines or armholes.
- Lay the back pattern piece on your fabric in the area designated for the back, add an additional 5 cm (2″) at the widest point, usually under the armhole, on both sides. Mark clearly.
- Add an extra 5 cm (2″) to both top and bottom of pattern, mark clearly.
- Draw a rectangle from these measurements, this is your jacket back ready to be cut.
- Using the same method, cut fronts and sleeves, but instead of adding 5 cm (2″) to each side add 2.5 cm (1″) with the length being adjusted as for the back.

Back:	Extra width —5 cm (2″) each side
	Extra length—5 cm (2″) top and bottom
Fronts:	Extra width —2.5 cm (1″) each side
	Extra length—5 cm (2″) top and bottom
Sleeves:	Extra width —2.5 cm (1″) each side
	Extra length—5 cm (2″) top and bottom

- Both upper and lower collars are cut 2.5 cm (1″) larger on all edges and are not shaped at this time.
- If you have chosen shoulder epaulettes, these are initially cut 2.5 cm (1″) larger than the pattern; both upper and lower epaulettes are interfaced.
- On all cut fabric pieces identify the right side of fabric and place a small strip of magic tape for ease of identification.
- Jacket pockets and facings are cut from the painted jacket fabric to pattern requirements.
- Interfacing for the jacket facings is cut according to the pattern. Interface both upper and under collar strips.
- To cut the dacron, lay silk pieces over dacron wadding.
- Rather than using pins (which are easily lost in the dacron) consider using the weights as described under equipment.
- Cut the dacron approximately 2.5 cm (1″) larger than the silk to allow for the take-up which occurs while quilting.

BASTING
The tradition of basting layers together with a

running stitch is time consuming and no longer necessary. With the availability of spray adhesives suitable for fabrics a light spray is all that is required over the dacron. Lay silk over sprayed dacron and leave to dry. It is not necessary to have all the edges etc. well adhered, just a light marrying of the two layers. *Do not* spray the adhesive directly onto the silk.

As a general rule of thumb the average jacket will require 4 to 5 full bobbins of thread, an all-over pattern 5 to 7 bobbins. If this number of bobbins is available to you, winding them before commencing quilting allows for a reasonably uninterrupted session.

Selective quilting. It is essential to quilt the design to be discernible, but do not overwork and eliminate the 'painted' quality of the work.

QUILTING

It is a good idea to start your quilting with the sleeves of the jacket; this allows you to get the feel of the painting you are working with and develop a flow with your work. The piece I am working in this section is a tree and cottage scene. My first consideration is to choose a line, running vertically to act as a holding line for my work. As I'm not one for unpicking, this line is chosen so that it will be part of the overall finished design. I have chosen the long vertical line running down the right hand side of the tree trunk, which not only provides good vertical hold but, being close to the centre of the piece, facilitates all further quilting, which is worked from this initial holding line. Working left of the initial holding line, I quilt the tree choosing only those lines that will add depth and volume to the painting. By far the biggest mistake of all beginners in this field is to over-quilt and end up with what I refer to as the 'chocolate box' look or grandmother's cushion.

Beware of over-quilting; it is immeasurably easier to add to your work should you feel it is under done, than perform the soul-destroying task of unpicking quilting lines and trying to camouflage machine needle holes. When quilting jackets I bar tack lightly at the beginning and end of each line; this is not noticeable in the overall finish of the garment. The other alternative is to pull the top threads through to the rear of your work and tie off.

Having finished the section to the left of the initial vertical holding line, I now move to the right and look for another vertical line to act as a holder for the right side. I have chosen the bush to the right of the cottage as this provides me with two further work areas, the centre between the two vertical lines and the extreme right. I then begin at the centre with both vertical and horizontal lines to work the cottage and the fence before moving over to the left.

The tree on the jacket back was quilted using the same principles, the initial vertical holding line being the large 'V' created by the trunk and large right-hand branch. In an all-over pattern one works the holding lines slightly differently by selecting an area in the centre of the work, quilting that section, then working outwards in a wide circle to the extremities of the fabric.

Having quilted the first sleeve to your satisfaction press lightly and place the sleeve dacron side down, lying flat until needed. Proceed with the second sleeve, both fronts and finally the back.

The important points to remember in quilting your jacket are:

1. Make sure areas such as neckline, armholes and the centre fronts have good holding lines.
2. Not all painted lines have to be quilted, indeed if you were to do so you will detract from the painting and end up with the 'chocolate box' effect.
3. Other people's quilting can be used for inspiration but remember quilting, like any art form, is a medium for self-expression.
4. Always create a centre holding line or area and work outwards from this point.
5. If you are not sure the line you wish to quilt is going to add to the value of your work don't quilt it, you can always go back and do so at a later stage.

Having completed quilting the five main areas check your work for loose threads on both sides. Thread snips are best for this work as you are less likely to snip the silk. Should this occur, and it does to all of us at some time, an extra quilting line is in order.

Now lay all your quilting out over a large area, the floor will do. Sit back and view your work. If you are feeling pleased with yourself you are entitled to, you have completed the most difficult phase of your jacket.

Next we quilt the collar. If your jacket is to have a stand up collar you quilt the under collar; if however your collar will be folded down you quilt the upper collar. The collar section you are quilting will have been adhered to dacron wadding. One of the following two principles will apply to quilting the collar.

1. If your collar has painted lines to follow, work to the same method as for the body of the jacket, exchanging the initial vertical holding line for a horizontal line. Exchange the technique of limited quilting for a good coverage, especially at collar centre front areas.

2. If you have chosen an unpainted area of silk for your collar, you will need to consider forming quilting lines to give an appropriate finish to the collar. The diagrams provide easy to follow examples. Do not, however, limit yourself to these ideas, experiment.

If you are having shoulder epaulettes, the technique for quilting is the same as for the collar.

CUTTING TO THE PATTERN

The jacket should now be cut to pattern requirements. I allow 1 cm seams for my jackets with the exception of centre fronts when inserting zippers; here I allow 2.5 cm (1″) because of the difficulty in finding location notches on the dacron. The only areas I notch when cutting are:

- Sleeve fronts and backs, always two for the back and one for the front.
- The pocket side edge and front side edges are notched for perfect insertion.
- Centre jacket back and centre collar.
- The lining is notched in a similar way.
- Having cut to the pattern requirements I then sew around all the edges of the cut fabric pieces. This prevents movement of the different layers, often in different directions, during construction.
- Any further notching required, i.e. the lower back, centre back and the lower band centre back, I do as I construct the garment.
- Very rarely do I use pins during the cutting process, I prefer weights.

Constructing the jacket

The instructions provided with your pattern will give you the step by step guide required to construct your jacket. What I attempt to provide here are the additional techniques used for the construction of quilted silk jackets; I also outline

Pressing the quilted collar

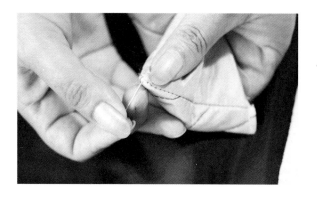

Pulling the collar to a fine point

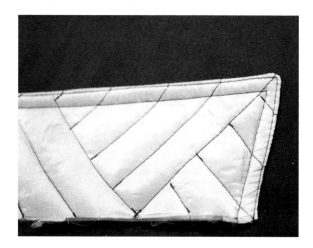

Top-stitching for finish

the sequence of construction and give hints I feel will be helpful.

COLLAR AND EPAULETTES

The collar, whatever your design, is still made in the traditional way:

- Upper to lower and stitched on the stitching line.
- Trim the seam allowance back to 1 cm.
- Trim dacron back to stitching line.
- Reduce bulk at corners by trimming corners diagonally.
- Curved edges are trimmed back carefully to a 3 mm edge (on the curve only).
- Well defined edges on a collar are obtained by first 'pressing open to press closed'. Before turning your collar press the seam allowance open. This is where your point presser comes into its own.
- Turn collar to right sides out, press.
- Press seams again, still flat, using the point presser.
- Now press the seams closed, coaxing corners with a pin if needed.
- Topstitch collar 7 mm from the outside edge, then a further row 1 mm from edge.
- Stitch the neck edges of collar together with a basting stitch.

Epaulettes are made in the same manner as the collar: press open to press closed and do not forget those points.

CUFFS AND BANDS

Should your design include these now is the time for construction. Bands for jackets are often made of leather, as these provide a frame for the painting. When making leather bands I use leather on the outside only and line the band with silk from the lining; the same method is also used on the cuffs. With leather one needs to use a pliable leather weld (available from leather skin outlets) to glue the leather seam allowance down on to the leather band. To obtain a good bonding with the weld, gently tap the glued leather edge on the wrong side with a rubber or wooden mallet; the wooden edge of a steak tenderiser works well. Follow the directions given on the pattern instruction sheet for the bands and cuffs; top stitch to match the collar and epaulettes. Should you consider making the jacket bands from silk, you will need to interface both band and lining and also consider quilting the band.

Epaulette top-stitched and completed with a self button trim

Leather bands faced with silk. This reduces weight and is economical of leather.

If you decide on this, a vertical quilting line is needed; adhere the dacron to the band, quilt and construct as for the collar. The photograph shows leather cuffs and bands with şilk cuff lining showing. The cuffs and bands in this photo have not been topstitched, and I recommend that you do so for a more professional finish.

FACINGS

Join front facing to back neck facing, press seam open. All seams are pressed open unless otherwise stated and excess dacron is trimmed from seam allowances.

LINING

- Join shoulder seams, press.
- Join left side seam from armhole to base and right side seam leaving a 13 cm (5″) opening at mid seam.
- Attach facings to lining. *Please note:* Sleeve linings are made separately and inserted with the jacket sleeves.

This jacket features an all over design of Australian gum flower. Creative quilting has identified the areas best left untouched whilst other areas are treated to detailed work. The sleeves received special attention with detailed stitching above the cuffs. The scarf was added to soften the appearance of this functional little jacket.

SLEEVE AND SLEEVE LINING (for jacket with cuffs only)

- Join sleeve seams, press using sleeve roll, insert sleeve roll into sleeve, press seam open with point of iron. Turn sleeve quickly and press again with sleeve roll in place.
- Attach cuffs to sleeve, trim.
- Press seam towards sleeve.
- Join sleeve lining seams, press.
- To attach the lining to the sleeve, the jacket sleeve is right side out, the cuff is turned back onto the sleeve exposing the joining seam.
- Right side to right side, lay the lining over the sleeve, ensuring front to front (check notches); the lining is then attached to the exposed sleeve/cuff seam close to the previous stitching line.
- Put sleeves to one side.

THE BODY

- Join shoulder seams, trim, press open.
- Using cotton tape for strength attach shoulder pads to front shoulder seam allowance.
- Attach pocket sections to jacket sides, matching notches.
- Flat stitch back pocket section close to seam.
- Join side seams leaving pocket opening free, trim seam, press.

ELASTIC-CASED SLEEVE

- Join lining to sleeve at lower edge, trim seam, press and flat stitch.
- Join underarm seams of sleeve and lining in one operation, upper edge of sleeve through to upper edge of lining, press seam using sleeve roll.
- Turn sleeve through to right side, press using sleeve roll.
- Fold elastic casing allowance back into sleeve, press, top stitch on right side 1 mm from edge.
- Stitch casing into place on seam line indicated *leaving a 5 cm (2″) opening for elastic insertion.*
- Insert elastic, join, close opening.
- Put sleeves to one side.

PLAIN SLEEVE (without cuffs or elastic)

- Follow instructions for elastic-cased sleeves.
- Instead of forming elastic casing, turn lining through, topstitch sleeve edge as for collar.

POCKETS

- Stitch pocket sections together, finish seams with over locking or zig-zag.

FOR SEPARATE BANDS ONLY

Attach lower band to jacket, trim seam (don't forget to remove excess dacron). Press seam toward jacket. Elastic casing at lower edge is constructed later.

FOR ALL JACKETS

- Insert sleeves into jacket (lining is left free). Check notches match.
- Trim seam, clipping as necessary, press towards jacket.
- Attach collar to neckline, trim, press seam towards jacket.

ATTACHING LINING AND FACINGS

- With right sides together, attach lining to jacket at front edges and neckline. Seams are trimmed, neckline clipped and pressed towards jacket.
- Corners are diagonally trimmed, front seams are trimmed and pressed open, use the point press.
- From the right side press the front seams closed.

ATTACHING THE SLEEVE LINING

- Pull the sleeve lining up through the sleeve, wrong sides together.
- Pin sleeve lining to jacket armhole seam (temporary hold only), ensuring notches and underarm seams match and sleeve lining is not twisted.
- Reaching from the open lower edge of jacket flip the jacket lining over towards jacket front, exposing jacket armhole seam.
- Now pin with linings wrong side together. (Previous pinning was to ensure the sleeve lining was lying correctly.)
- With all notches and seams matching stitch seam, clip as needed, press seam open.

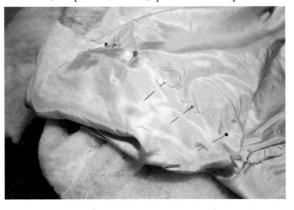

Setting the line prior to closing

JACKET WITH SEPARATE BANDS

- Turn jacket, right sides together.
- Join the lining to the jacket at lower edge, stitching inside the band seam, trim.
- Clip corners diagonally, press seam towards jacket.
- Jacket is turned back through opening in side seam of lining. If using studs do not close the lining. If buttons are to be used, slip stitch opening together.

JACKET WITH LOWER ELASTIC CASINGS

- *Note:* I recommend that two separate side casings be used. Proceed as for jacket with bands. After turning jacket through to right side, measure casings 13 cm (5″) both sides of side seam (two of 25 cm (10″) each).
- Top stitch lower edge of this measurement 1 mm from edge, stitch upper casing line, same measurement.
- Reaching through side opening in lining thread elastic into casing, pinning securely to hold.
- Stitch elastic from right side, with two rows of stitching 5 mm apart.

JACKET WITHOUT BANDS OR ELASTIC CASINGS

- Proceed as for jacket with bands. Once jacket is turned through to the right way press lower edge closed.
- Top stitch lower jacket edge to match lower sleeve edge.

CLOSURES AND FINISHING

- If a zipper is to be used, the zipper is stitched into the jacket fronts before shoulder seams are joined.
- Jacket is then constructed in normal manner.
- Once facings and linings are inserted the linings are flat stitched onto the zipper seam allowance.
- Outside topstitching is done at the end of construction.
- Studs (snap fastenings) are attached as per manufacturer's instructions with the added

Final top-stitching with closures; in this case self buttons of matching material

insurance of placing 2.5 cm (1″) square of leather between dacron and facings. This gives extra bite for the stud and prevents damage to the silk.
- Use the opening in the lining side seam to insert the leather squares.
- Slip stitch lining together at completion of studding.
- Buttonholes are made in the normal manner; you may find a piece of tissue paper inserted between machine bed and fabric will prevent feed problems.
- Press thoroughly.

While this project is hard work it is very satisfying and the end result looks and feels fabulous.

*Fold upon fold of dazzling colour. Draped silk painted
by Louise Feneley.*

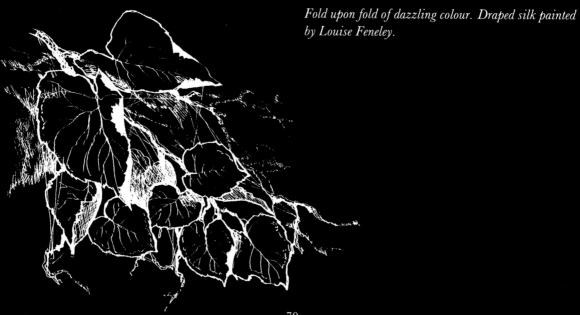

8
The story of silk
Jacqui Robertson

*J*ACQUI *is a director of Sericus Pty Ltd, an Adelaide company specialising in importing and wholesaling silk fabrics. In this role she has established links around the world, with silk suppliers in China, Asia and Europe whom she visits regularly.*

She has developed a strong knowledge of silk fabrics and works closely with a textile chemist in her relentless pursuit of quality.

Sericus Pty Ltd is currently the sole Australian member of the International Silk Association.

THE NAME 'silk' comes from the old English word *sioloc*, which is thought to have originated from the Greek word *seres* meaning people from Eastern Asia, probably referring to the Chinese.

Often described as 'nature's miracle fibre', silk may be regarded as the most valued of the natural fibres. Due to its great tensile strength—5.1 gm per denier (65 000 lb per square inch—the same as that of mild steel)—and the length of each filament (commonly 90 metres) the 'queen of fibres' has great versatility. It can be woven to make the sheerest of fabrics which seem to float. Individual filaments can be combined to form a single, much thicker yarn of the weight most commonly used in garments, where the continuous nature of the yarn imparts a unique sheen. It can also be used as a short staple fibre, and spun like cotton or wool.

The production and weaving of silk (sericulture) has been carried on for several thousand years. It began in China, where it was a closely guarded secret. Over the centuries eggs were smuggled out of China (in a head-dress to Kashmir, in a hollowed-out walking stick to Byzantium) and centres of sericulture were established in Japan, India, the Middle East and Europe.

Silk can be obtained from a wide variety of moths (about 400 species in all), but the finest is obtained from the cocoon of the caterpillar of the moth *Bombyx mori* when fed on the leaves of the white mulberry tree, *Morus alba*.

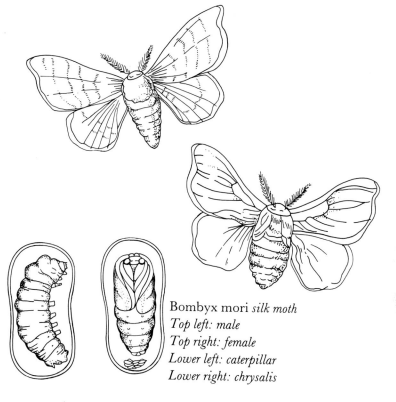

Bombyx mori *silk moth*
Top left: male
Top right: female
Lower left: caterpillar
Lower right: chrysalis

Bombyx mori, unknown in the wild state, is believed to have been native to China. The newly hatched caterpillar is black or dark grey and covered with tufts of long hair. These are lost at the first moult, and the caterpillar becomes creamy-white, with a brown head and a horn on the eighth segment of its abdomen. When fully grown it is about 7.5 cm long. It converts most of the albumen content of the mulberry leaves into liquid silk which it stores in its body.

When mature and ready to spin its cocoon the caterpillar exudes a little of the silk solution through two glands (spinnerets) on either side of its head, finds an anchorage, and then stretches the thread out by drawing back its head. It builds an oval casing around its body by moving its head in arcs, crossing in figures of eight, to add layer after layer. In 24 to 72 hours its protective covering, the cocoon, is completed.

The finished cocoon measures about 4 cm in length and is either shining white or yellow, depending on the caterpillar's race. Some races of silkworm breed once a year (uni-voltine) while others have two or more generations (multi-voltine). The finest silk comes from the caterpillar of uni-voltine moths.

The enclosed silkworm undergoes a transformation from caterpillar to inert chrysalis or pupa. The coating of the chrysalis is hard and yellowish brown. While it appears lifeless it is sensitive to the touch. It develops rapidly into a moth which, when ready to emerge, secretes a fluid to cut an opening through the cocoon and the silk that surrounds it.

The moth is whitish grey, with a soft body but no mouth, and does not eat. It has lost the ability to fly, and its short adult life of 1 to 4 days is entirely for reproduction. The female moth lays about 500 eggs, and in so doing completes her life cycle.

In sericulture only a sufficient number of moths to ensure the next season's crop is allowed to emerge from the cocoon. The rest are 'stifled' while in the chrysalis state to preserve the continuity of silk thread around the cocoon. Stifling is generally done using heat, by baking the cocoon in an oven. It can be done by refrigeration, when the chrysalis is not killed but held dormant.

The cocoon thread, known as the bave, comprises two filaments, or brins, of silk fibre (fibroin) which are held together and coated by silk gum (sericin).

One ounce (28 gm) of eggs yields 35 000 larvae, which eat half a tonne of mulberry leaf, producing 25 000 cocoons, from which 56 lb (25 kg) of stifled or 14 lb (6 kg) of reeled silk may be obtained. One ounce (28 gm) of silk is about 100 000 yards (91 500 m) in length. The cocoons of 100 silkworms, weighing about 1 lb (450 gm), yield about 1.5 to 2 ounces (40 to 60 gm) of best silk). The remainder is made into spun silk. It takes about 5000 silkworms to produce the silk for one kimono.

The silk filaments are reeled off the cocoon into hanks at a silk-reeling establishment, called a filature. The cocoons are sorted by type, size, colour and district, and all double, waste, thin and stained cocoons are removed. The cocoons are shrunk in preparation for unwinding and reeling by being placed in a cooking bath where the temperature is carefully controlled. During this operation they are sprinkled with cold water, condensing the steam inside, and causing them to shrink. This allows water to enter the cocoon during reeling, adding enough weight so that all the figure-eights of the filament, as originally spun by the silkworm, will be straightened out.

Reeling

For reeling the cocoons are steeped in hot water to soften the silk gum and free the fibre. They are then brushed to remove the outer web or casing and pick up the outside of the filament. A sufficient number of threads (commonly 4 to 6) are pulled up together to form the thickness of raw silk thread desired, and passed through porcelain guides. Two sets of threads are then twisted around each other in a process known as the crossing or 'crossieur'. This consolidates the filaments, pressing them into a uniform and compact thread. It also cleans from them any impurities and dries them. It is essential that the same number of cocoons are kept in action to give

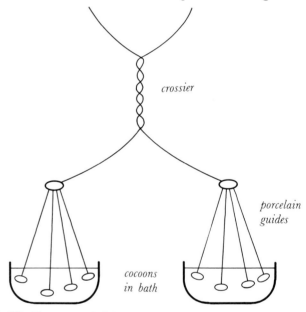

Silk filaments reeled from the cocoons to produce a filature

evenness of thread, so if a filament breaks it must be replaced immediately. Many faults which show up in cloth are the result of bad reeling.

Some of these faults are:

Waste: A mass of tangled open fibre attached to the raw silk threads.

Nibbs and slubs: Thickened places several times the diameter of the thread.

Split threads: Large loops, loose ends, or open places where one or more filaments are separated from the thread.

Knots: These appear where broken filaments are tied up. The ends should not exceed 3 mm in length.

Throwing

From the filature the silk is taken to the throwing mill.

The term 'throwing' comes from the Anglo-Saxon word *thrawan*, meaning to twist or spin. Thus the word here means to twist the silk. The throwster converts the raw silk thread into a yarn of the proper size for manufacturing, or, by regulating the twist, produces various qualities of silk yarn for weaving or knitting.

SORTING
When the silk is received from the filature the 'book' or bundle of raw silk is opened up and the smaller bundles or 'mosses' are examined. The mosses (or skeins) are sorted into grades according to colour and cleanness, i.e. freedom from inequalities such as knots or loose ends.

The silk is soaked in an oil or soap emulsion to soften the thread without dissolving the gum. It is then wound onto bobbins and several threads are doubled together to give the desired size of yarn, and then twisted.

WINDING
The silk is wound from the skeins onto bobbins or reels.

CLEANING
The silk thread is passed through a very sharp double knife, the edges practically touching, to clean off all unevenness and hairy filaments.

THE FIRST THROWING
This is equivalent to the spinning operation for other textile fibres and consists of twisting the filaments together by means of a flyer system. The amount of twist inserted depends on the purpose for which the yarn is to be used. Some yarns are given as many as 60 twists to the inch in the first throwing process. After the first throwing the yarn is called 'singles', although it contains 12 or more single filaments. The term 'dumb singles' describes the yarn before throwing.

DOUBLING
Here two, three or more threads are wound together to increase the thickness and strength. This is done without twist.

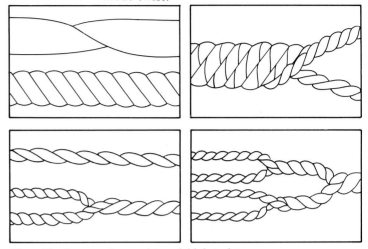

Top: Single yarn, low twist and high twist
Top right: 4 ply yarn
Bottom left: 2 ply yarn and single yarn
Bottom right: Cord yarn

SECOND THROWING
This is similar to the first throwing, but twist is inserted in the opposite direction, thus binding the threads together into a compact yarn.

STEAMING
The thrown silk is steamed to set the twist.

SIZING
The silk is graded for size and quality.

REELING
The thrown silk is reeled onto large metal drums to be stored until required. When silk leaves the throwing mill it is still in the gum and is called 'hard silk'. It is still in this state when woven into cloth—the gum strengthens and supports the thread during the weaving process.

Classification of fibres and thrown silk yarns

DUMB SINGLES
Fine silk threads reeled without twist and combined to form tram or thrown weft silk. This is also known as *net silk*.

TRAM
Two or more dumb singles, doubled and with just sufficient twist to hold them together. They are

twisted as little as possible in order to retain their lustre and filling power. They are generally used for weft silk.

COMPENSENE YARN

A right and left crepe yarn, each having 40 to 50 turns to the inch, are twisted together with about 5 turns per inch. This gives a balanced yarn which will not kink while being knitted.

ORGANZINE

Two single threads each twisted 16 turns left, doubled and twisted 14 turns right. This yarn makes excellent warp stock.

GEORGETTE

Two or three untwisted singles, doubled and twisted 70 to 75 turns right and left and used as filling yarn in weaving.

SEWING SILK

Made from 10 to 15 raw silk threads of 14 denier size formed in two and three ply. The criterion of strength is given by the product of yards per ounce and the breaking strength in pounds. The minimum standard is 6000 units.

EMBROIDERY SILK

Consists of a number of simple untwisted threads united by a slight twist.

ECRU

Thrown silk with only a little of the gum taken away. The term applies to silk cloth before being degummed.

SCHAPPE SILK

A term sometimes used to describe spun silk, but takes its name from the Schappe method of degumming, where the silk is put into vats of warm water below boiling point and left for some days or even weeks, and is allowed to ferment.

FLOSS SILK

A soft yarn with very little twist used for embroidery. Also used to describe a type of waste silk.

BAVE

A double filament of raw silk.

BRIN

Single separated filament of raw silk.

DOUPPIONS (DUPIONS)

Silk reeled from double cocoons or cocoons produced by two caterpillars. It is hard to reel and produces a very slubby raw silk fabric.

Waste silk

There are two major classifications:

THROWSTER'S WASTE

This is produced when the raw silk thread is converted into a woven or knitted fabric, i.e. during winding, twisting, warping, quilling, weaving or knitting.

GUM WASTE

This comes from the primary market of rearing silkworms and reeling raw silk thread.

These wastes are divided into types according to the method of their production and are kept segregated as to origin.

FLOSS

The tangled mass of silk on the outside of the cocoon which is valuable owing to its purity and fine size, although it has a high gum content.

FRISONS OR KNUBS

The long waste produced in finding the end of the cocoon filament to start the reeling operation. Also called waddings or blaze, it is full of gum and consequently lacking in lustre. It contains long sections of filaments of excellent quality, but must be carefully dried at the filature to avoid hard 'heads' or masses of fibres held solidly by the silk gum when it sets.

CURLIES OR FRISONETS

The waste produced during reeling as short portions of the filament are unwound before making the 'cast-on'.

PIERCED COCOONS

These are obtained from the egg-producing establishments, where the moths are allowed to emerge for reproduction purposes. This source of gum waste is one of the best for spun silk manufacture.

THIN AND STAINED COCOONS

These are not reelable for raw silk, and are an inferior type of waste.

PELLETTE

The pellette or inner parchment-like skin is the residue of the cocoon after reeling and the cocoons dropped during the reeling process. They are the least desirable forms of silk waste.

NERI OR RICOTTI

This is a term sometimes used to denote the waste inside the cocoon.

Spun silk

Waste silks are collected in bales, to be opened as required. Pierced cocoons and frisons are opened and placed in large kettles containing soap solution, rinsed and dried. Clean waste is lapped or pulled, filled and freed from short fibres and foreign matter in a dressing mill and formed into flags.

These short fibres are usually classified into four grades:

1st quality: Average fibre length 6.5 inches (3–10 in.) (17 cm)
2nd quality: Average fibre length 4.5 inches (2.5–6 in.) 11 cm)
3rd quality: Average fibre length 3.5 inches (2–6 in) (9 cm)
4th quality: Noils—the short fibres at the end of the cocoon yarn, often with pieces of cocoon still attached. They are spun into coarse yarn on special machines. This yarn was once used mainly for insulation. Noils are also used in the making of weaving yarns and are mixed with wool.

Clean long-staple fibres are formed into wide ribbons (laps) and drawn in a gill box to form a sliver. Slivers are doubled and drawn a number of times to give a thorough distribution of fibres before twist is inserted to produce finished spun silk yarn. As spun silk is produced from a mass of broken, fine fibres it is convertible into a great variety of interesting weaves. Great care is taken in blending to provide strength by combining the longer fibres with the shorter ones. Spun silk produces fabrics with soft, pliable finishes.

SILK COUNTS

Raw silk is known by its 'title' or count, which is the weight in deniers of 450 metres of raw silk, one denier being equal to 0.05 gm. The double thread produced by the silkworms counts about 2.5 deniers when in the gum, so that a single filament would count about 1 denier, after degumming. Net silk is usually quoted as 12/14, 16/18, etc. and sold on the middle or average figure, i.e. 13, 17 deniers etc. It is very unusual to find two hanks weighing (i.e. counting) exactly the same. If a single filament counted exactly one denier then a silk thread with a title 13/15 would contain 13 to 15 filaments.

This method of counting silk threads is the most usual and is the legal standard upon which other methods are based. The count of spun silk is calculated in the same way as cotton, i.e. the number of hanks each measuring 840 yards that it takes to weight 1 lb avoirdupois.

The structure of silk

To understand the behavioural characteristics of silk, both its advantages and its limitations, it is helpful to have some understanding of its basic structure.

When viewed through a microscope, de-gummed mulberry silk resembles a smooth transparent rod. If still in the gum its surface looks rough and irregular and it feels quite stiff. Wild silks (tussah, etc.) are more uneven in appearance, and thicker, than cultivated silk. They are also darker due to the presence of tannin in the fibre (which comes from the tannin in the leaves eaten by the silkworms). In all other ways the micro-structure of these silks is the same.

THE MACRO-STRUCTURE OF SILK

It is a fine regular translucent filament. The diameter of the fibre may vary from 1.2–3.0 microns, depending on the diet and origin of the silkworms. Thus it has a length to breadth ratio of 2000:1.

The beauty and softness of silk's lustre is due to the smooth triangular cross-section of the filament, which when twisted in a yarn results in a fibre with subdued sheen.

Linear fibroin polymers in a folded configuration

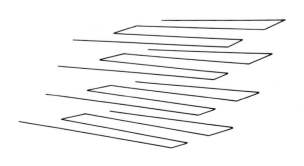

THE MICRO-STRUCTURE OF SILK

The fibre is a fine coagulated stream of fibroin. Fibroin is a linear polymer composed of 16 different amino acids. None of the amino acids contains sulphur, thus it is a system containing no disulphide (covalent) bonds; this lack of covalent bonds between the acids affects the behavioural characteristics of the fibre. The polymer system is thought to be composed of folded linear polymers, which lie along the fibre, and this explains why its structure is estimated at being 65%–70% crystalline and 35%–30% amorphous.

The strength of the filament is due to this linear configuration and its very crystalline polymer system which permits the formation of many hydrogen bonds in a regular manner.

Silk is considered to be more plastic than elastic as its regular crystalline structure permits less reversible movement than would be possible in a more amorphous system. If stretched excessively the polymers slide past each other so that when the stress is removed the polymers remain in their new positions, now amorphous. The resultant disorganisation can be seen as distortion and wrinkling in the fibre.

Silk is sensitive to heat because the bonds of the polymer system tend to break down when excessive amounts of heat/kinetic energy are applied to them.

Silk is a hydrophilic fibre with a moisture regain of 11%. Under normal conditions 11% of the weight of the fibre is its moisture content, thus water is an essential part of the fibre's make-up. This may be one of the reasons that silk does not support a flame—the latent heat required to convert the water content to steam would absorb much of the heat energy of the flame. The moisture absorption of silk is around 35%, i.e. it will absorb up to that amount of its weight in water before it feels wet. This is one of the reasons that it is such a comfortable fibre to wear. When silk is fully saturated, however, its strength is reduced by half. The bonds between the polymers are hydrolised and weakened. Its full strength returns when it is dry. This means that care needs to be taken when handling silk while it is wet; avoiding too much strain on the fibres, or abrasion to them.

The fibre is readily degraded by mineral acids, to which it has no resistance due to the lack of disulphide bonds between its constituent amino acids. This sensitivity to acids means that silk garments worn next to the skin should be washed after each wearing to remove perspiration which is acidic. The fibre is tolerant of organic acids, and immersion in a weak solution of acetic acid (without rinsing) is commonly used to impart 'scroop' to silk fabrics.

When silk filaments are exposed to alkali they swell, due to the separation of the polymers by the molecules of the alkali. Silks yellow and colours are dulled after incorrect washing and this happens because alkaline detergents cause a re-arrangement of the surface polymers of the filament. Thus, it is essential that a non-ionic, non-alkaline cleaner is used to launder silk.

The low resistance of the silk filament to prolonged exposure to sunlight is due to the ultra-violet rays causing the bonds between the polymers to sever. The degradation resulting from the breaking of these bonds causes a change in the reflectivity of the filament, as well as a weakening of the filament structure. Similar damage is done when the fibre is subjected to chlorine bleaches.

The depth of colour obtained when silk is dyed is due to the structure of the filament. The translucency and smoothness of the fibre mean that it will reflect truly any colour placed in it, with very little distortion due to surface dispersal of incident light.

The highly crystalline structure of silk resists small distortions, giving the fibre excellent crush resistance. Creasing may result when these distorting forces exceed the resilience of the crystalline structure, and when heat is applied, causing a re-alignment of the polymers.

Silk is a highly durable cloth due to its resistance to biological and fungal attack. Throughout history silk has been recognised for its comfort, elegance, durability and luxury, and it has always been highly prized. Not for nothing is it known as the 'queen of fibres'.

9

From yarn to cloth

Jacqui Robertson

THE FUNCTION of any yarn is only fully realised when it is woven (or knitted) into cloth. Therefore no study of any fibre would be complete without an examination of at least the most common of the weaves in which it is used.

When fabrics are woven they are produced in units whose length will vary according to the weight and width of the weave or fibre. These are commonly referred to as pieces. Weaves that are very heavy or extraordinarily complex may be produced in pieces as small as 10 metres whilst sheer lightweight pieces may be as long as 100 metres.

FABRIC WIDTHS
Excluding ribbons, tapes and braids, fabric widths vary tremendously—from 30 cm up, according to local traditions or as a function of the limitations or possibilities of a particular yarn.

FABRIC WEIGHTS
Weights of fabrics vary enormously. Although they are often expressed as grams per running/linear metre (gm), it is more informative to specify weight per square metre, as any difference in width does not then affect a comparison. These latter weights are usually listed as grams per square metre (gm/sq m), or for silks momme per square metre (m/m). A momme, roughly equivalent to 4.33 gm, is a traditional Japanese weight for both silk and pearls.

The weight of a fabric affects its suitability, durability and cost, and should always be borne in mind when selecting cloth. It can vary from as little as 15 gm/sq m (or 5 m/m) to 600 gm/sq m (140 m/m) or more.

The lightest fabrics can only be constructed from yarns with both strength and fine spinning qualities, such as silk. Super-light fabrics can be expensive due to the cost of processing very fine yarns. Medium weight fabrics are generally cheaper as they are produced using standard yarns in standard weaves. Heavy material tends to be dearer due to the extra yarn used and possible complications in weave structure.

Deciding which weight of silk (or other fabric) to use for any purpose invariably involves a compromise between appearance, performance and cost.

Woven fabric structures

A simple woven fabric is composed of two series of yarns called warp and weft which are interlaced at right angles. The warp runs along the length of the fabric, and the weft across from selvedge to selvedge. The weight, appearance, texture and stability of the fabric result from the thickness, nature and composition of yarns used, together with its structure, i.e. the closeness of the yarns in the weave, and the frequency of the inter-lacings. Finishing processes may also have some effect on fabric performance.

The manner in which the yarns are interlaced gives rise to a particular weave and the regularity of its repetition is known as its 'repeat'. The size of the repeat will depend on the size and complexity of the pattern woven into the fabric.

Just as there are the three primary colours, so there are three primary types of weave and all woven fabrics are a variation of these weaves. Plain, twill and satin weaves each have their own variations and the combinations between them place an enormous variety of woven cloth at our disposal.

PLAIN WEAVE
Plain weave is the simplest form, and variety is obtained by different thickness and texture of yarn, and closeness of warp and weft. Three plain weave variations known to most of us are rib, cord and hopsack.

In a rib weave there are visual lines of construction across the fabric. A cord weave produces

lines along the length of the fabric. Hopsack is a plain weave doubled, i.e. the yarns interlace in pairs, rather than singly.

Above: When one thinks of silk the images are soft flowing fabric which shimmers, luscious to the eye and *touch. It comes as a surprise to consider that this fibre can be worked into any configuration of weave and that it is possible to have denim and corduroy made from silk. The most commonly hand painted silk is light weight. These are readily available examples.*

TWILL WEAVES

Twill weaves all possess the characteristic of diagonal lines across the fabric. The simplest twill is produced by stepping one yarn space to the right of each successive warp/weft interlacing. This weave enables yarns to be woven closely, making a compact yet supple fabric. The direction of a twill can be either warp or weft, depending on whether warp or weft yarns are used as the floats. (A float is any yarn, warp or weft, which is carried over more than one opposing yarn in the fabric before being interlaced in the weave.)

A 2/2 (2 warp/2 weft) twill is often used for suitings, and can be implemented in various ways: in herringbone twill the direction of the twill is changed regularly to form the pattern. When weft and warp threads are equally spaced and of equal thickness, this twill presents an equal number of warp and weft threads to the front and back face of the cloth.

If the balance between warp and weft is altered, cloths of very differing wear characteristics will result. This is done with jean cloth (2/1 twill) and drill (3/1 twill) which are woven to present a solid hard-wearing warp surface. In weft twills the softer weft threads are floated on the surface for textural or lustrous effects. As a result they are not so hard wearing. Looseness of weave will start to show if the floats are made to span more than three opposing yarns.

The direction of the diagonal in an equal twill is 45 degrees. If the balance is altered, or if there is a difference in thickness between warp and weft yarns, the direction of the diagonal will change. The angle increases noticeably in drill, due to its 3/1 balance, and in gaberdine, which is a 2/2 twill where the warp yarns have been brought closer together and the weft yarns decreased in frequency. Regardless of the angle of the twill the line of the true bias of the cloth is always 45 degrees because the warp and weft remain at right angles to each other.

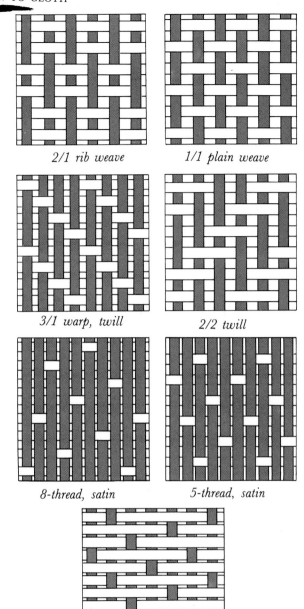

2/1 rib weave *1/1 plain weave*

3/1 warp, twill *2/2 twill*

8-thread, satin *5-thread, satin*

5-thread, sateen

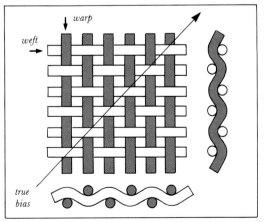

Woven fabric : plain weave

Weaving patterns produce the unique appearance and individual character of the cloth.

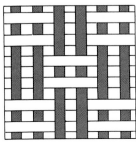

2/2 hopsack weave

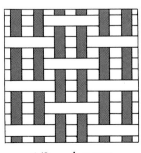

1/2 cord weave

SATIN WEAVES

Satin weaves are structured to produce a smooth lustrous surface. The face of the fabric is predominantly warp. A satin is often described according to its coverage, as in a 5-thread satin where each warp yarn passes over 4 weft yarns and under one. The warp yarns are set almost twice as closely as the weft yarns so that each single weft interlacing is hidden by the adjacent warp floats. If the structure is correctly set it will give the impression of a smooth unbroken surface. Plain satins are a one-sided fabric, the reverse side being quite coarse in structure.

The long floats in satin expose the filaments to damage from abrasion in both making-up and wearing. A cheap satin usually lacks closeness in its structure and is therefore subject to slippage and cracking, i.e. an opening-up of the weave.

Sateen is a weft-faced satin weave, i.e. the weft yarns are more closely set than the warps, and are floated over the warps.

These three basic types of weave can be used individually or in combination to create an almost limitless variety of weaves.

JACQUARD

Jacquard is a term used to describe a complex cloth with a regular self-pattern woven into the fabric as a result of hundreds of different interlacings. All the basic weave types discussed earlier are involved in jacquard fabrics.

This patterned fabric takes its name from a machine first exhibited at the Paris Exhibition of 1801 by Joseph Jacquard. Looms on which these complex weaves are produced still bear the name of Jacquard, and a typical small machine would have 200 hooking mechanisms. These allow the weaver to have control over 200 warp yarns, permitting the weft to be woven into the cloth, above or below any of the warp yarns, as desired. The instructions for the interlacing pattern are punched onto cards, one for each weft yarn inserted. The cards are tied together in a continuous loop, and in this way the pattern is continuously repeated. In recent times magnetic tape or computer programs are taking over from punch cards to control jacquard looms.

Selecting silk fabrics

When choosing a fabric for a particular function it is essential that its stability is examined with regard to its proposed purpose. The significant factors to look for are yarn thickness and texture together with yarn spacing and the frequency of interlacing between warp and weft.

RECOGNISING SILK

It is usually sufficient to be satisfied by the feel and general appearance of a fabric. However, if you are doubtful that a fabric really is silk, the classic burn test, on a small piece, will confirm or deny your suspicions. (Do not use matches as the phosphorus in the match-head will confuse your sense of smell.) Insert the piece in the flame: silk will burn reluctantly and will stop burning when removed from the flame. It will give off a smell rather like burning feathers (similar to wool, but more unpleasant). A glossy black residue will crush to a fine powder if rubbed between your fingers. If the silk has been weighted with metallic salts it will behave in much the same way, but will glow in a skeleton of the weave.

Now look at the closeness of the weave, and compare the weave with how the fabric feels in your hand. If it is an open weave and feels quite stiff it may well have been treated with a stiffening agent, i.e. sized. A sizing treatment may be water soluble, so if you were to wet the silk it would change in behaviour and become quite floppy. Sizing may affect a silk's ability to take silk paint as desired by the artist.

One way of 'improving' a poor silk, which should be guarded against, is to soak it in sodium alginate. This is done to make a poor weave feel 'full'. The moment such a silk is washed, its true nature will be revealed and all appearance of substance will vanish. You can usually tell if this has been done to a fabric by close examination of the weave using a magnifying glass or microscope. If the interlacings of the yarns are not 'clean', i.e. there is filling matter between the fibres, it is a possibility. This sort of treatment is very different from the sizing mentioned in the previous paragraph, because the motivation behind it is disguise rather than effect.

FABRIC TYPES AND FABRIC RECOGNITION

The appearance, texture and handle of a fabric are the clues to identifying it. Listed below are a few fabrics of the kind more commonly used by silk painters.

CHIFFON

Chiffon is a plain weave. It is made from highly twisted fine yarns, woven in a very open structure. The twist in the yarns is in the same direction. The cloth is woven in gum condition and degummed after weaving. Although thin and sheer it is fairly strong, but may give at the seams. It is often decorated with a satin spot or satin stripe. It has beautiful handle and excellent draping qualities. Given that it is so light, it is quite strong. It is recommended for loose fitting garments, such as overdresses for evening wear. It can be difficult to handle when making up. If the edges will not lie straight when cutting out, pin the fabric to sheets of paper using very fine pins or needles to avoid making holes in the fabric. Scissors need to be very sharp. When sewing on a machine a needle sized 70–80 is recommended, with synthetic thread. Use a small stitch with a slight zig-zag to add some give to the seams. A piece of tissue paper placed underneath the fabric helps prevent wrinkling under the foot of the machine. As chiffon frays easily all raw edges should be enclosed in French seams or similar. It is very transparent and so all edge finishing should be shell, roll or binding.

CREPE DE CHINE

Crepe de chine is a plain weave. The warp is softly twisted while the weft yarns have a high twist and are set in alternating pairs of S and Z twist (i.e. left-twist and right-twist) causing a cockling of the fabric weft-way. It is a fairly crisp lustrous fabric with good draping qualities due to its softly twisted warp. It was Coco Chanel who brought this fabric 'out of the boudoir'! It was originally used only for lingerie and linings, but since Chanel shocked the world it has been very popular for blouses. It is usually washable and is quite easy to make up. A machine needle of 70–90 is recommended, with a medium stitch with slight zig-zag. All weaves made with crepe yarns fray easily, so it is a good idea to hold all raw edges together with oversewing or French seams.

CREPE GEORGETTE

Crepe georgette is a plain weave using hard-twisted yarns in both warp and weft. The yarns generally alternate in pairs, i.e. two S yarns, two Z yarns. The result is a very springy fabric with a strong crepe effect (sometimes described as 'pebble'), and good drape and handle. Due to its springiness it can be difficult to make up. It is usually handled in much the same way as crepe de chine, and often used for blouses and dresses.

GEORGETTE

Georgette is a plain weave filmy fabric with a crepe appearance. It is often confused with chiffon. The difference is that, as with crepe georgette, the alternating yarns are hard-twisted in opposite directions. The resultant fabric is springy and light and hardly creases at all. In cutting out it needs to be handled carefully as it is inclined to move. It is easier to handle than chiffon. It frays readily so all edges should be enclosed. It is ideal for soft full floaty styles, and gathers well. A needle size 70 is recommended for machine sewing, with a small stitch.

JAP SILK

Jap silk is a thin, almost papery, silk fabric of plain weave, made from net silk yarns. It has characteristic irregularities in both yarn and weave, particularly in the weft. Traditionally used for lining lightweight garments, its lack of strength and durability make it unsuitable for outer clothes. It has become popular with silk painters because the lack of twist in its yarns results in colours having maximum lustre and sheen. It is very light and slippery to make up, and tends to move when cutting. Scissors need to be sharp. When machining use a needle size 70–90, a small to medium stitch, and silk or synthetic thread. It can be bought under various names—paj (which is simply jap reversed), China silk, the name by which it was originally known, and it is sometimes incorrectly called pongee.

PONGEE

Pongee is a plain weave silk fabric made from wild silk (tussah silk) yarns. It has a slightly rough feel and excellent draping qualities. This fabric is ideal for blouses, dresses and nightwear. When machining use a needle size 70–80 and a small to medium stitch. The stiffness which can often be felt in this fabric when new is thought to be due to the higher wax content present in tussah silk, and will disappear after a few washes.

HABUTAI

Habutai is a term meaning soft and light, and describes a soft, lightweight, plain weave silk excellent for linings. It is popular with silk painters and has greater dimensional stability than paj. Its yarns are thicker and, having a light twist, it has slightly less lustre. In its heavier weights this fabric makes excellent shirting. When machining use a needle size 80 and a medium stitch, with either silk or synthetic thread.

FOULARD

Foulard is a twill weave in silk, which is now more commonly sold simply as silk twill. It is traditionally used for soft-styled dresses and blouses, scarves, men's light dressing-gowns etc. It takes colour beautifully, and deserves to be more popular with silk painters. As it is soft and floppy it can be quite difficult to handle. The fabric needs to be cut carefully as it will easily move from the straight position. It frays quite readily so all raw edges should be enclosed. It drapes and gathers well. As with other slippery fabrics, a piece of tissue paper placed under the seams when machining should help prevent wrinkling. When machining use a synthetic thread and a needle size 70–80 with a small to medium stitch.

TAFFETA

Taffeta is a closely woven plain weave fabric made with net silk yarns. It has a stiff handle and a characteristic rustle. Traditionally it was woven 'square', so that it was faced with an even number

'Protea' by Di Teasdale. This painting makes full use of the dispersing effect produced by applying water to a painted surface.

of warp and weft yarns. It is now also woven with the warp yarns more closely set than the weft, producing a faint rib effect across the fabric. It is not hard-wearing, so it has been traditionally used for evening wear, stiff petticoats, lampshades, cummerbunds, artificial flowers, linings, etc. It is not easy to sew and is a fabric that creases easily. Garments should not be tightly fitted but, if they are, the seams should be supported by stronger fabric. When machining use a needle size 70–80 with a small to medium stitch and synthetic thread.

Silks should be sewn using a fresh needle for every new garment. The silk fibre is very strong so the needle point needs to be sharp enough to spear its way through the fibre. A blunt needle can cause ugly pulls in the fabric.

10
Dyestuffs and dyeing
Jacqui Robertson

WHEN A FABRIC is coloured to a particular hue the refractivity of the fibre is changed, either by chemical change to the fibre itself, or by covering the fibre with a substance of a different refractivity.

Colouring matters fall into two groups—dyestuffs and pigments. A dyestuff is a soluble compound which, when processed and applied to the fabric, penetrates the fibres or combines with them, changing their colour. A pigment is an opaque insoluble compound which is applied to the surface of the matter to be coloured and chemically bound to it, changing its colour. In silk painting both dyestuffs and pigments can be used.

The first dyestuffs were derived from living materials and are therefore described as organic dyestuffs. Most now available commercially are synthesised (synthetic organic) or come from mineral sources such as coal and tar (inorganic).

The dyestuffs used in proprietary silk paints will have been selected with ease of application being the primary consideration, sometimes at the expense of other more desirable characteristics. The vast majority will belong to two general classes—acid dyestuffs and direct dyestuffs. Each brand of silk paint will have its own proprietary mix of reagents added to the dyestuff in the solution you purchase, enabling you to paint it directly on to the silk surface with little or no preparation, thereby shortcutting the dyeing process for which the dye base was originally prepared. When you steam your work you are completing the dyeing process.

The steam permeates the fabric, water droplets adhere to fibre, giving you a 'mini dyebath' around each fibre. The heat of the steam causes the fibre to swell, enabling the dye molecules to get inside. More precisely the added kinetic energy creates more movement and vibration among the molecules, causing them to move further apart, creating temporary voids in the fibre which allow further penetration of the dye molecule. The dyestuff stays in the fibre by means of molecular attraction (or chemical reaction), causing its colour to change more or less permanently.

Fastness

The permanency with which the dyestuff will remain bound to the fibre is extensively tested by the manufacturing chemical company. Some dyestuffs can photochemically degrade, i.e. the dyestuff is altered by exposure to light, so, while still present in the fibre it transmits no colour. The tenacity shown by a particular dyestuff under controlled conditions is described as its colour fastness and this will be ascertained for a large number of different circumstances. A numbering system is used to describe it. Fastness to light is rated on a scale of numbers from 1–8; other fastness properties on a scale from 1–5. The higher the number the better the fastness. Ideally we should restrict our use to those dyestuffs at the top of these scales.

Fastness properties vary greatly between the families of dyes, and between the colours in those families. When manufacturers of dyestuffs issue their colours they accompany them with an enormous amount of detailed information relating to their fastness properties.

Fastness properties will govern the use to which a dyer will put a particular colour. To take an extreme case, a dyer would not choose a dyestuff with low wet fastness or low light fastness to dye fabric designated for swimwear.

Fastness properties are critically dependent on the temperature and time factors in operation when the fabric is dyed. Perhaps it is the lack of control in the non-laboratory setting which causes most brands of silk paints to withold information regarding the fastness properties of the colours in their range. If the information were available the silk painter could be guided when selecting colours for specific garments.

Types of Dyestuff

Most of the dyestuffs used on silk come from those developed for other fibres which also have an affinity for the silk fibre. It is from these that your silk paint will have been produced. In general they will fall into three main groups, the first two being the most commonly used.

DIRECT DYESTUFFS

Direct dyestuffs are so called because they have a direct affinity for cellulosic fibres such as cotton. Some of them also have an affinity for the silk fibre. They come in a wide colour range and are easy to apply. They are fixed with steam and appear much the same colour after steaming as when first painted on the silk. Their disadvantage is that in general they have low wet fastness and some have low light fastness. (Manufacturers are moving to replace the affected dyes with substitutes based on different chemical formulations.)

ACID DYESTUFFS

Acid dyestuffs have a direct affinity for protein fibres (silk and wool). The colours in this range are more intense and brilliant than direct dyestuffs, but in other respects they are similar. Some acid dyestuffs have moderate light fastness, and poor to fair wet fastness. The pre-metalised dyestuffs produced by some companies have greater fastness, though they are less brilliant than acid dyestuffs. Steaming is required to fix the colour.

FIBRE-REACTIVE DYESTUFFS

Fibre-reactive dyestuffs, as their name suggests, react directly with the fibre. At some point during the procedure an alkali is added to initiate the chemical reaction.

Their fullest intensity is achieved with cotton, but they perform well on silk. They possess a greater degree of both light and wet fastness than acid or direct dyes, but are more difficult to use. They are often labelled as a cold water dye, and are applied in two parts. If a dye calls for the use of washing soda as a fixative you know it belongs to this group. They require special handling: the solution cannot be stored for any length of time. Once the dye is mixed with water it will slowly lose its potency, and will not fix on the fabric despite the fact that the solution still possesses its full colour brilliancy.

Apply these dyes a shade darker than you actually desire, because a small percentage of the dye will sit on the fabric without reacting with it. These dyes can be fixed by steam or cold fixed.

Cold fixing of the colour involves the addition of an alkali preparation of a pH value high enough to cause a reaction between dye and fibre. Cold fixing in this way is not highly desirable for silk as the silk fibre is very easily damaged by alkalis.

In steam fixing reactive dyes you add a weak alkali (sodium bicarbonate) to the dye solution just before applying the 'paint' to the fabric. During steaming the heat breaks down the sodium bicarbonate to form a more alkaline compound which triggers the chemical reaction between dye and fibre.

VEGETABLE DYESTUFFS

Until synthetic dyestuffs were first developed in the mid 19th century, all dyestuffs came from natural sources. The extraction of dyestuffs from natural materials requires considerable work, often just in finding the source material, let alone in preparation. Their application often involves the use of mordants. These are chemicals used to treat the fabric so it will accept the colour as required. A different mordant used with the same vegetable dye can result in a different colour. Many of the mordants used in natural dyeing are hazardous and should be used with extreme care by experienced dyers only.

PIGMENTS

Pigments differ from dyestuffs in that they are insoluble in water, opaque, and instead of penetrating the fibre the finely ground particles lie on the surface and are bound to it. They have the advantage of being bright, but some are extremely susceptible to crocking (i.e. rubbing off). There are fabric paints commercially available which are pigments suspended in a resin-type binder. They are usually set by heat: ironing or tumble drying. Due to their plastic sheen they are very rarely used by silk painters.

Precautions

All dyestuffs, whether natural or synthetic, are active chemicals and should be respected as such. Treat them with the same degree of care and commonsense you would use when handling any other chemical:

- Always wear rubber gloves, or use a barrier cream, to prevent possible absorption of dyes through the skin.
- After working with dyes scrub the hands and nails with soap and water. Do not use bleach, as this will break down the skin's natural defences.
- If working with dyestuffs in a powdered form work on dampened paper—this will trap most spillage.
- Powdered dyestuffs can be hazardous if inhaled, so work in a draught-free environment and replace caps on containers immediately.

- Once utensils have been used for handling dyestuffs they must be reserved for that use only.
- Work in a well ventilated area to avoid the possibility of inhaling any vapours.
- Do not smoke or drink while working with dyestuffs.
- Dispose of concentrated dyestuffs thoughtfully: do not pour them down the drain into the sewerage system. You are being much more environmentally conscious if you throw them onto a patch of garden, where the constituent chemicals can slowly leach their way through the natural filtration system of the soil over many years.

Multi-media

Having allocated so much space to explaining some of the many diverse techniques by which white silk can be converted to colour, I would like to expand further by including some fine examples of multi-media. These were painted by Di Curtin from Wollongong, New South Wales.

Faerie people *painted on porcelain and silk which was then embroidered in silk thread.*

The small fairy in shadow was painted on porcelain. Silk was overlayed and cut away to expose her. The silk painting was then developed around this area. Small threads were drawn from the silk to depict grasses. The picture was completed by extensive embroidery about the base of the tree.

The lamp was designed so that the base and shade are extensions of each other. Faerie creatures are a favourite subject of Di's. The atmosphere created in this piece is delightful. Perfect use is made of the translucent silk and porcelain to depict the twilight world of these creatures.

Brambles *by Di Teasdale.*

Compared to the pieces above my small foray into experimentation appears feeble. This piece is a combination of antifusant and coloured guttas painted onto pongee silk. This silk is quite thick and has a slub which produced a pleasing texture but made painting difficult.